# Photoshop
# Effects
# Magic

D1314963

# Photoshop Effects Magic

BY RHODA GROSSMAN

# Photoshop Effects Magic

Library of Congress Catalog Number: 96-78986
ISBN: 1-56830-344-0

Copyright © 1997 Hayden Books

Printed in the United States of America 1 2 3 4 5 6 7 8 9 0

## Warning and Disclaimer

## Trademark Acknowledgments

| | |
|---|---|
| **President** | Richard Swadley |
| **Associate Publisher** | John Pierce |
| **Publishing Manager** | Laurie Petrycki |
| **Managing Editor** | Lisa Wilson |
| **Marketing Manager** | Kelli Spencer |

## The Photoshop Effects Magic Team

**Acquisitions Editor**
Jawahara Saidullah

**Development Editor**
Beth Millett

**Copy/Production Editor**
Terrie Deemer

**Technical Editor**
Kate Binder

**Publishing Coordinator**
Karen Flowers

**Cover Designer**
Aren Howell

**Book Designer**
Gary Adair

**Manufacturing Coordinator**
Brook Farling

**Production Team Supervisors**
Laurie Casey, Joe Millay

**Production Team**
Trina Brown, Dan Caparo, Billy Huys, Christopher Morris, Scott Tullis, Megan Wade

# Hayden Books

The staff of Hayden Books is committed to bringing you the best computer books. What our readers think of Hayden is important to our ability to serve our customers. If you have any comments, no matter how great or how small, we'd appreciate your taking the time to send us a note.

You can reach Hayden Books at the following:

Hayden Books
201 West 103rd Street
Indianapolis, IN 46290
317-581-3833

Email addresses:

America Online:   Hayden Bks
Internet:              hayden@hayden.com

Visit the Hayden Books Web site at http://www.hayden.com

# About the Author

**Rhoda Grossman**

Rhoda is a freelance illustrator and cartoonist whose work has appeared in numerous publications on digital art, including Hayden Books' *Photoshop Creative Techniques* and *Fractal Design Painter Creative Techniques*.

Whether in her Sausalito studio or teaching or doing caricature demonstrations as Rhoda Draws A Crowd, she combines hi-tech and lo-tech art and refers to herself as "bi-tech."

She finds time to work for artists' rights and is the founder of AAARGH, Artists Against Arbitrary Regulations and Government Harassment.

Rhoda has a 4-year-old computer, an 11-year-old car and a 28-year-old daughter, all working. You can find her at: http://www.digitalpainting.com.

# Dedication

For Sherry London, who led me down the garden path.

**Special Thanks to...**

Sharron Evans for teaching me cool techniques.

Marc Schmid, Barbara Pollack, and Liz Beatrice for contributing artwork, even if it has to wait for Volume 2.

Roy Gordet for his generous gifts of time and legal advice.

Diane Fenster and Helen Golden, for being my role models.

Melanie Rigney, who made me an offer I couldn't refuse, Beth Millett for knowing whether to crack the whip or the joke, and the rest of the Hayden Team.

My mother, Ida, whose jello made the "Saturation" technique possible...and whose love made me possible

The folks at Adobe who have created the software that if I were marooned on a desert island and could only have one graphics application I would pick if only I could answer the question, "where do I plug this in?"

# Contents at a Glance

# Contents

# Introduction

Photoshop users at all levels will find this book a tasty reference. There are easy-to-use recipes for producing all the looks you see as you thumb through these pages. You'll find techniques for working with photos and with line art...and quite a few ways to create something from nothing. The CD-ROM that accompanies this book contains an assortment of photos, drawings and other tidbits. These can serve as ingredients for the recipes, but you are encouraged to find and create your own as well.

So, this isn't just a cookbook, though you could use it that way. It's more like a 42-course dinner. You could eat your way through until you're stuffed, and still come back for seconds. Or you could just nibble and pick.

There's a tempting smorgasbord of effects for digital illustrators, designers and fine artists. Don't worry, I haven't forgotten the "Sunday Painters" though I guess I'd better call them "Weekend Digitizers."

Whatever your reasons for using Photoshop—commercial assignments, personal creativity, or simply "because it's there," put down that knife and fork, and pick up your mouse or stylus. Now, dig in!

Rhoda Grossman

# Before You Start

## Welcome

Welcome to another volume in the series for creating "Magic" with Photoshop. Like its sisters, *Photoshop Type Magic* and *Photoshop Web Magic*, this book is more than a how-to manual—this book is a what-to guide. The steps in this book tell you exactly what you need to do in order to create exactly what you want. Flip through the thumbtabs to find the effect you want to create and follow the concise, explanatory steps. Or thumb through to discover an effect you never imagined and learn what to do to create it. If you need a little extra help, flip to the Photoshop Basics section. But, before you jump in, let me tell you a little about how this book works. A quick read now will maximize your time later.

## System Setup

Here are the system recommendations for creating these effects.

MacOS users: The Adobe Photoshop 4.0 Info box suggests a memory allocation of 21 megabytes (MB) of RAM to run Photoshop. And your system software may need as much as 10MB of RAM. That's a full bowl of soup, but if you've got the memory, then I would recommend setting the Preferred memory size even higher than 21MB. If you don't have 21MB to spare, quit all other applications and give it everything you've got.

Windows users: Adobe suggests 32MB of RAM for Photoshop on any 386 or faster processor running Windows 3.1, Windows 95, or Windows NT, but 40MB is better. Quit any application you can before starting Photoshop to maximize the running of the application. Photoshop runs 32-bit native on both Windows 95 and Windows NT operating systems.

It is not crucial, but it will help if you have a CD-ROM drive. A number of the effects in this book use files contained on the CD-ROM that comes bundled with this book. (See Appendix B, "What's on the CD-ROM," for information on accessing those files.) However, even if you don't have a CD-ROM drive, you still can perform all of the effects described in the book.

## Adobe Photoshop 4.0

All of the techniques in this book were created with Adobe Photoshop 4.0, and that's the version I recommend you use. If you're attempting to duplicate these techniques using an earlier version of Photoshop, your results may differ slightly or significantly compared to mine. If you're working with version 3.0, you still will be able to create all of the effects in the book. Keep in mind, however, you will need to adjust the instructions for the differences between the two versions. You will see that even some of the old Photoshop features work differently in Photoshop 4.0. Many of the effects in this book use features not available in earlier versions of Photoshop.

## Conventions

Every image in this book was created initially as an RGB file. You can make your effects in any appropriate color mode, but you should be aware of the variations this will cause as you proceed through the steps. The first new channel created in an RGB file, for example, is automatically named Channel #4. But the first new channel created in a CMYK file is named Channel #5. You also should be aware of the differences in the color ranges of the various color modes. Some colors that look great in RGB mode may look like mud after you convert the file's color mode to CMYK. The Lighting Effects filter, for example, will not work on a CMYK or grayscale file.

If you'd like more detailed information about the different color modes, refer to a good general Photoshop book such as *Photoshop 4 Complete* or to your Photoshop user manuals.

Also, every image was created as a 150-dpi resolution file. (The thumbtab images were created as 300 dpi files.) If you are going to work in a resolution other than 150 dpi, remember that some of the filters and commands will require different settings than the settings I used. Because there are fewer pixels in a 72 dpi image, a Gaussian Blur radius of 5 pixels will blur the image more than if it were a 150 dpi image. Just keep an eye on the figures next to the steps and match the outcome as close as you can.

I used a pressure-sensitive digitizer tablet and stylus to create all the images, but a mouse works fine for most of them. A tablet is suggested for best results with the "Impressionism," "Cloning," "Burning Type," "Bristle Brush," "Quick Color," "Rough Sketch," and "Textured Brush" techniques.

## The Blue Type

As you work through the steps, you will see phrases colored a light blue. These same phrases are listed in alphabetical order in the Photoshop Basics section. If the phrase in blue asks you to perform a task you are unfamiliar with, you can find that phrase in the Photoshop Basics section and follow the instructions on how to perform that task.

## Menu Commands

You also will see instructions that look like this:

Filter➡Blur➡Gaussian Blur (2 pixels)

This example asks you to apply the Gaussian Blur filter. To perform this command, click on the Filter menu at the top of the screen and drag down to Blur. When Blur is highlighted a new menu opens to the right, from which you can choose Gaussian Blur.

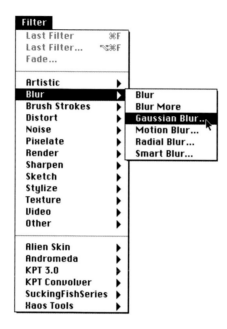

In this example, a dialog box appears asking you for more information. All of the settings you need to perform each task appear in the text of the step. The previous example tells you to enter 2 pixels as the Radius.

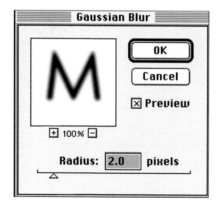

Click OK to blur the image.

3

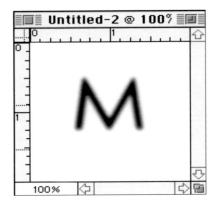

## Settings

Following each action in the steps, you will find the settings for that feature. These recommended settings are meant to act as guides; the best settings for your effect may vary. As a rule, it is best to match the outcomes that you see in the figures as you progress through the technique. The greatest differences occur when the resolution of your file is significantly different from what I used. The following two images demonstrate the importance of adjusting for resolution differences. A 6-pixel radius Gaussian Blur was applied to both images.

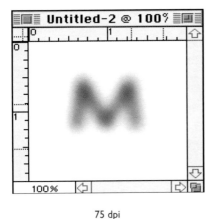

75 dpi

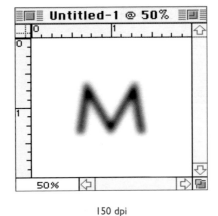

150 dpi

## Tips

Throughout the book, you will find additional bits of information that can help you make the most of Photoshop. These tips provide information beyond the basic steps of each lesson.

# Photoshop Basics

The goal of this section is to help new and novice users of Photoshop with the simple, basic tasks required to create the effects described and illustrated in this book. Each of the basic tasks described in this section corresponds to the blue highlighted text in the chapters that follow. Here, users can easily find the instructions they need for performing a particular Photoshop task.

This chapter proceeds on two assumptions: that you're creating my effects in Photoshop 4.0; and that you're keeping the Toolbox, and the Brushes, Options and Layer/Channel/Path palettes open. If one or more of these palettes are closed when you refer to this chapter, you can reopen them by name by using the Window menu at the top of the screen. If you're using an earlier version of Photoshop, you can refer to the Photoshop manual for instructions on how to perform these tasks.

## The Toolbox

If you're not familiar with Photoshop's toolbox, there's no reason to panic. With a bit of experimentation, it doesn't take long to learn each tool's individual functions. This representation of the toolbox will help beginners and experts alike find the tools they need.

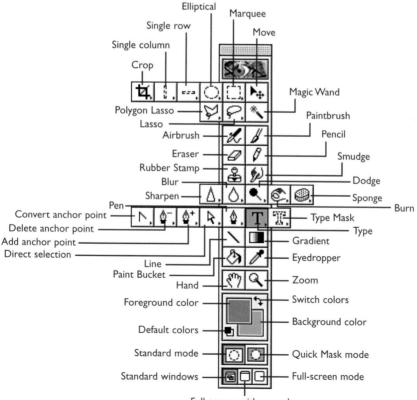

## Basic Photoshop Tasks

### Choose a Foreground or Background Color

**Shortcut**: Press D to change colors to their defaults: black for the foreground, and white for the background.(Note: if you are working on a layer mask, pressing D will give you white foreground and black background.)

Press X to switch the foreground color with the background color.

To change the foreground or background color click on either the Foreground icon or the Background icon.

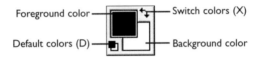

The Color Picker dialog box appears, which enables you to choose a new foreground or background color by moving and clicking the cursor (now a circle) along the spectrum box, or by changing specific RGB, CMYK, or other percentage values. Note that the Foreground and Background icons on the Toolbox now reflect your color choices.

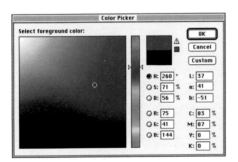
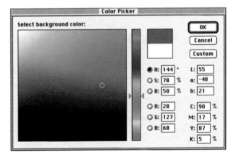

### Convert to a New Mode

To convert from one color mode to another, click on the Image menu at the top of the screen and scroll down to the Mode command. You then can scroll down to select the mode of your preference. If you want to switch from CMYK mode to multichannel mode, for example, you choose Image➡Mode➡Multichannel. The check mark to the left of CMYK will move down to Multichannel, indicating that you are now in multichannel mode.

**TIP** Remember that there is a different range of colors available for each color mode. No matter what color mode the file is in onscreen, for example, your printer (if it prints in color) is going to print your work in CMYK. Because the color ranges for RGB and CMYK are different, you should convert your RGB image to CMYK before printing. Otherwise, you may be in for a big surprise when your bright green prints as a dull tan.

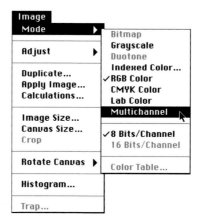

## Create a Layer Mask

To create a layer mask, click the Layer Mask icon at the bottom of the Layers palette. A layer mask is used to mask out (or hide) parts of a layer. Painting with black hides an area, and painting with white reveals it. Dragging a layer mask to the trash icon at the bottom of the Layers palette allows you to apply it or delete it. Here the layer mask is active, indicated by the black border around it and the mask icon in the active layer.

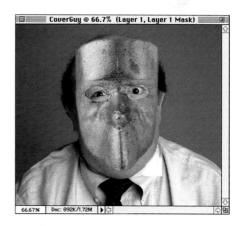

### Create a New Channel
**Shortcut**: Click the New Channel icon on the Channels palette.

To create a new channel, choose New Channel from the Channels palette pop-up menu.

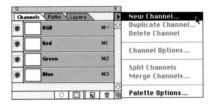

Use the Channel Options dialog box to establish your settings. Unless noted otherwise, we used the default settings when creating a new channel. This figure shows Photoshop's default settings.

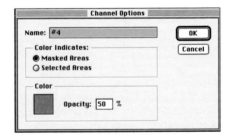

### Create a New File
**Shortcuts**: Press (Command-N)[Control-N].

To create a new file, choose File➞New. The New dialog box appears, which is where you name your new file and establish other settings. See Part I, "Before You Start" for information on the conventions that were used when creating new files for the type effects in this book.

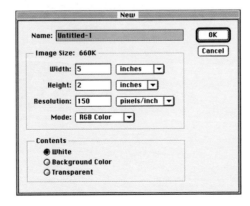

## Create a New Layer

**Shortcut**: Click the New Layer icon on the Layers palette.

To create a new layer, choose New Layer from the Layer palette pop-up menu, or choose Layer➡New➡Layer.

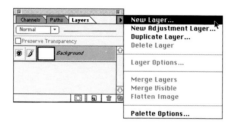
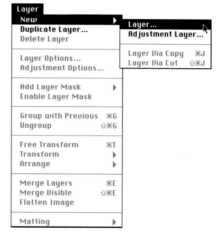

The New Layer dialog box opens, which is where you name the new layer and establish other settings.

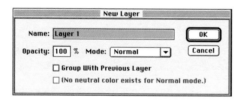

## Delete a Channel

To delete a channel, go to the Channels palette and select the channel you want to delete; drag it to the Trash icon at the lower-right corner (just like you would to get rid of a document on the Desktop for Mac users). You also can select the channel you want to delete, and choose Delete Channel from the Channels palette arrow menu.

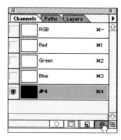
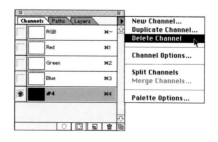

## Deselect a Selection

**Shortcut**: Press (Command-D)[Control-D].

To deselect a selection, choose Select➡None. The marquee disappears.

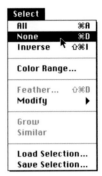

## Drag and Drop

This technique *is* a shortcut. It eliminates copying to and pasting from the clipboard. With two images open, select an area from the source image and drag it over to the destination image, using the Move tool. A new layer is created automatically.

**Shortcut**: Press (Command)[Control] to access the Move tool.

## Duplicate a Channel or Layer

**Shortcut**: Click the channel or layer you want to duplicate, and drag it on top of the New Channel or New Layer icon.

To create a duplicate of a channel or Layer, make it active and then select Duplicate Channel or Duplicate Layer from the appropriate palette pop-up menu.

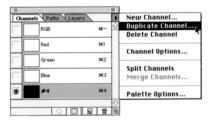

A new copy of the channel you selected for duplication is created automatically, and the Duplicate Channel dialog box appears.

## Enter/Exit Quick Mask

**Shortcuts**: Press Q to enter and exit the Quick Mask mode.

Click the Quick Mask icon to switch to Quick Mask mode; conversely, click the Standard mode icon to return to Standard mode.

Essentially a Quick Mask is a temporary channel. When you're in Quick Mask mode you can use any of the Photoshop tools and functions to change the selection without changing the image. When you switch back to Standard mode you'll have a new selection.

## Enter the Text

Before entering the text using the standard Type tool, make sure that the foreground color is set to your desired text color. If you are entering text into a layer, then the standard Type tool will create a new layer for the type.

To enter the text, select the Type tool, and then click anywhere in the image to open the Type Tool dialog box. Type the text in the large box at the bottom of the dialog box, and make your attribute choices from the options (listed previously). Unless noted otherwise in the instructions, always make sure that you have the Anti-Aliased box checked.

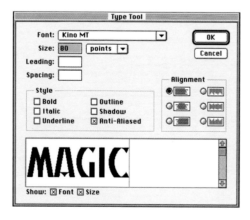

After clicking OK, move the type into position with the Move tool.

## Fade the Effect

**Shortcut:** (Shift-Command-F)[Shift-Control-F] opens a dialog box for fading the last filter used and changing its blending mode.

To fade the last Filter applied, or some other effects such as Invert, choose Filter➡Fade.
The Fade slider acts like a partial undo for the last effect you applied. The Blending
Mode pop-up menu enables you to determine how the pixels of the before and after
versions of the image are combined.

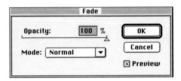

## Fill a Selection with Foreground or Background Color

First, select the foreground or background color you want to use (see page 18 in
this section for instructions). Keep the selection active and press the (Option-Delete)
[Alt-Backspace] keys to fill the selection with the foreground color. If you are in the
Background layer or any layer that has the Preserve Transparency option turned on, then
you can press (Delete)[Backspace] to fill in the selection with the background color.

You also can fill in your selections by choosing Edit➡Fill, or press (Shift-Delete)
[Shift-Backspace] to open the Fill dialog box.

This causes the Fill dialog box to appear, enabling you to establish the Contents option
you want to use, the Opacity, and the Blending Mode.

**TIP** If a selection is empty (a transparent area of a layer) and the Preserve Transparency option is turned on for that layer, then you will not be able to fill the selection. To fill the selection, simply turn off the Preserve Transparency option before filling it.

## Flatten an Image

To flatten an image (merge all the layers into a single layer), choose Flatten Image from the Layers palette arrow menu, or choose Layer➡Flatten Image.

## Load Brushes

To load another library of brushes, choose Load Brushes in the Brush palette pop-up menu. You can choose whether to "append" additional brushes to the default library or replace the defaults. I recommend you append the Assorted Brushes that come with Photoshop. I've also included a few custom brushes in the Presets folder on the CD-ROM that comes with this book.

13

# Photoshop Effects Magic

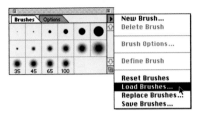
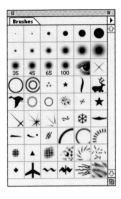

## Load a Selection

**Shortcut:** Hold down the (Command)[Control] key and click the channel (on the Channels palette) that contains the selection you want to load.

To load a selection, choose Select➡Load Selection. This brings up the Load Selection dialog box, where you can establish document, channel, and operation variables.

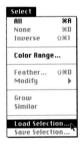
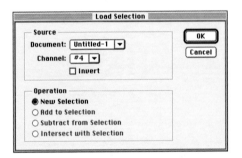

14

## Make a Channel Active

To make a channel active for editing or modification, click on its thumbnail or name on the Channels palette.

You can tell the channel is active if it is highlighted with a color.

## Make a Layer Active

To make a layer active, click on its thumbnail or name in the Layers palette.

You can tell the layer is active if it is highlighted with a color.

## Make a Layer Visible/Invisible

To make a Layer visible or invisible, click in the left-most column in the Layers palette. If an eye appears, then the layer is visible. If the column is empty, then that layer is hidden (invisible).

## Move a Layer

To move a layer's position in the list, click on the layer you want to move in the Layers palette and drag it up or down the list of layers to the place you want to move it. As you drag the layer, the lines between the layers will darken to indicate where the layer will fall if you let go.

## Name/Rename a Layer

To change the name of a layer double-click its name in the Layers palette and type the new name in the Layer Options dialog box.

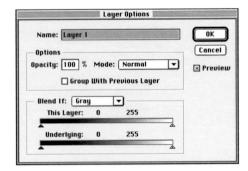

## Place an Image

Use File➡Place to bring an EPS (Encapsulated PostScript) image into an open Photoshop document. The image will appear in a bounding box which can be manipulated before anchoring with a click of the (Return)[Enter] key. A new layer is created automatically with the name of the EPS file.

## Return to the Composite Channel

**Shortcut**: Press (Command-~)[Control-~].

If you want to return to the composite channel, click on its thumbnail or title (RGB, CMYK, Lab). The composite channel always will be the one with (Command-~)[Control-~] after its title.

If you are in an RGB file, then Channels 0 through 3 should now be active because each of the R, G, and B channels are individual parts of the RGB image.

## Save a File

To save a file, choose File➡Save As. This displays the Save As dialog box, where you name your new file and choose a format in which to save it.

File format selection depends on what you have in your file, what you want to keep when you save it, and what you're going to do with the file after it is saved. Consult a detailed Photoshop book, such as *Photoshop 4 Complete*, for more guidance on which file format is best for your needs.

 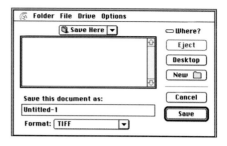

## Save a Selection

**Shortcut**: Click the Save Selection icon on the Channels palette.

To save a selection, choose Select➡Save Selection.

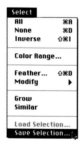

The Save Selection dialog box opens. Choose your options and click OK to save the selection.

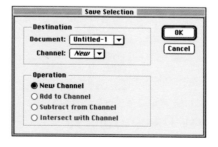

17

## Switch Blending Mode

In many techniques you will be instructed to change from Normal to another blending mode. This may refer to the Options palette for some tools, or the Layers palette, or the Fade dialog box. Blending mode influences how the pixels from two sources will combine.

# Photoshop Effects Magic

To change from Normal mode to any of 16 alternatives, first click the pop-up menu and then drag to your choice of mode. Consult your Photoshop User Guide for details on how each blending mode works.

## Switch Foreground/Background Colors

**Shortcut**: Press X to switch the foreground and background colors.

To switch the foreground and background colors, click on the Switch Colors icon. This flips the two colors shown in this icon only, and does not affect the rest of the image.

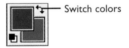

Switch colors

## Switch to Default Colors

**Shortcut**: Press D to switch to the default foreground and background colors.

To change the foreground and background colors to black and white respectively, click on the Default Colors icon.

Default colors

## Turn On/Off Preserve Transparency

To turn on or off the Preserve Transparency option for a particular layer, first make that layer the active layer. Then, click the Preserve Transparency checkbox on the Layers palette. This option is not available for the Background layer.

## Vary Pressure

If you are using a graphics tablet and pressure-sensitive stylus you can vary the brush size, color, or opacity as you paint by varying your pen pressure; check the appropriate boxes in the Options palette for a tool to vary any or all of these three characteristics.

If you are using a mouse, you can specify a number of steps in the Fade field to make a stroke that feathers out. The higher the number of steps, the slower the fade.

Changing the value on the Opacity slider is effective for both mouse and tablet users.

19

# PART I

# Working with Photos

Why can you no longer use photographs as evidence in court? Why can't you believe the pictures you see in the tabloids? Photoshop is why.

You'll find techniques here for enhancing reality, combining two or more realities and distorting reality beyond all recognition. You'll learn how to add color, reduce color, and alter color in a wide variety of ways. You'll see how to create artistic effects, old-fashioned styles, and some truly terrifying looks I wasn't sure what to call.

The "Impressionism" and "Cloning" techniques work much better if you have a graphics tablet.

Source photos are provided on the CD-ROM. Use your own photos if you prefer. In fact, why not scan family portraits, take digital snapshots at the office party…you begin to see the possibilities?

Photoshop's Layer Mask feature enables you to create a gradual transition between two or more images. First we will compose some simple fades, and then build to a thrilling climax with "Chainlink Symphony." All images used in this section are in the Digital Stock➡Urban Textures folder of your *Photoshop Effects Magic* CD-ROM.

**1** Open the images "Hirise" and "Cans."

**2** In "Cans," Select➡All, then copy and paste the image into "Hirise" where it becomes Layer 1. Hirise is now the background.

By reducing the opacity of Layer I
to 50% you achieve the simplest
kind of blend.

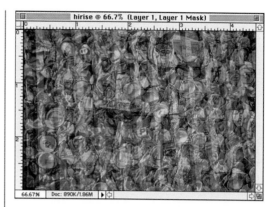

**3** Create a layer mask for Layer I
("Cans"). You'll use it to create
more complex blends.

**4** Double-click the Gradient icon
and use these settings in the
Gradient Tool Options palette.

**5** Switch to default colors. Drag the
Gradient tool vertically from the
top of the image to the bottom.
Your Layers palette will show a
white-to-black gradient in the Layer
Mask.

At 100% opacity and in Normal mode the composite image looks like this.

What a compelling image! Recycling cans into building materials…or, modern cities being buried in garbage—it's your choice.

# VARIATIONS

## Horizontal Blend

For this variation, I copied the Railing image into the Door image, and created the layer mask in Layer 1 as done previously.

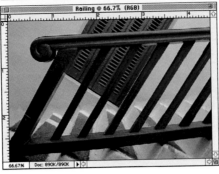

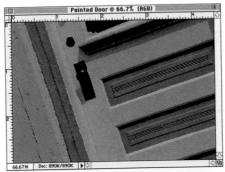

Gradient Tool Options are the same as before. To make the images fade from right to left, drag the Gradient tool horizontally in Step 5. To make the railing fully visible on the left and fading out to the right, the layer mask needs to have black on the right and white on the left.

 **TIP** Remember "black conceals and white reveals."

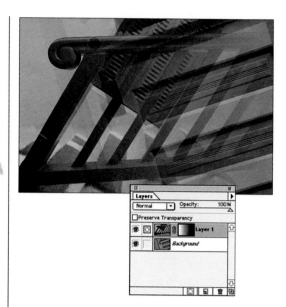

## Radial Blend

For this variation, I copied the Chainlink R (red) image into the Chainlink Y (yellow) image, and created the layer mask in Layer 1 as done previously.

25

In the Gradient Tool Options palette, I set the type of fill for radial and dragged the gradient from the center to the edge.

Let's create a new layer and add it to the radial blend of red and yellow.

Open "Chainlink B" (blue) and Copy it to the red and yellow composite, where it becomes Layer 2. Create a layer mask and drag a linear gradient diagonally from the lower-left corner to the upper-right corner.

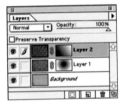

How would the composite look if we changed the blue layer to a radial blend and the red layer to a diagonal linear blend? Layer masks make it easy to try multiple variations before making up your mind.

1 Drag each of the layer masks to the Trash icon in the Layers palette. Choose "discard" when you are asked whether to apply the masks.

2 Create another layer mask for the blue layer. Apply the gradient as in Step 5 of the Radial Blend variation.

**3** Repeat Step 8 for the red layer.

I reduced the opacity of the blue layer to 76%, and liked the result. ■

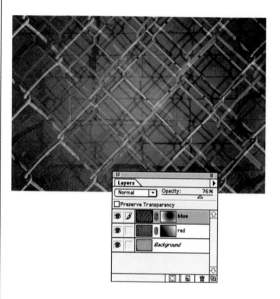

A border or decorative edge can be the finishing touch to your photo or artwork. The Border command in the Select➡Modify pop-up menu is only one of the ways to get the edge. Many variations result from your selection choices, stroke and fill options, feathering, filtering, and colors.

## Flat Borders

The simplest kind of border is a solid stroke or fill.

**1** Open the image you want to work with. I'm using "Houses" from the Urban Textures collection in the Digital Stock folder on the *Photoshop Effects Magic* CD-ROM.

**2** Choose a background color for your border. I picked up the light tan color from the window trim with the Eyedropper tool (CMYK 19, 23, 39, 2). Use Image➡Canvas Size to add space around the artwork. This space fills with the background color.

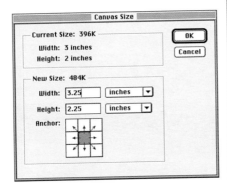

**3** To add a contrasting stroke, choose a foreground color. I picked up orange from the image with the Eyedropper tool. Make a rectangular selection where you want the stroke and use Edit➥Stroke. Choose the width and placement of the line. Mine is 4 pixels and drawn outside the selection.

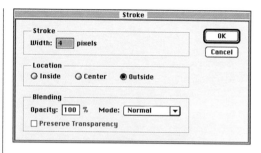

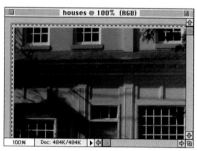

**TIP** To assure accurate positioning of the stroke, select the image inside the border and use Select➥Modify➥Expand. Enter the number of pixels for enlarging the marquee. Your new selection is perfectly centered. View➥Show Rulers and View➥Show Grids may be helpful too. File➥Preferences gives you options for units of measure and grid spacing.

## Feathered Borders

Make a selection and use Select➥Modify➥Border. Specify how many pixels wide, and Photoshop automatically feathers both sides of the selection. I began with Select ➥All to eliminate the outer feathering, creating a kind of vignette. For more examples, see "Vignette" (page 108).

The Border command also works on elliptical and free-form selections. Here's "lollipop" from the Digital Stock folder on the CD-ROM.

**1** Make a freehand selection with the Lasso tool.

**2** Choose a background color. Use Select➡Inverse to make the area outside the "marching ants" active. Press Delete to fill the selection with background color.

**3** Choose a foreground color. I picked up the golden yellow of the lollipop with the Eyedropper tool. Use Select➡Inverse again.

**4** Use Select➡Modify➡Border and specify width in pixels. I used 24. Fill the selection with the foreground color.

## Fancy Borders

**1** Open the image you want to work with. I'm using "Cameras" from the Image Club folder on the CD-ROM.

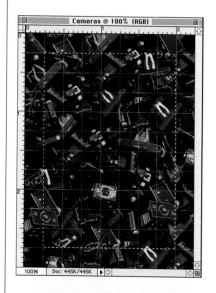

**2** Drag the rectangular Marquee to select the area you want to be inside the border. I'm using a grid to help make my border symmetrical. Feather the selection. I used **24** pixels. The rounded edges of the "marching ants" marquee indicates feathering.

**3** Use Select➡Inverse to make the area outside the "marching ants" active.

31

**4** Apply a filter effect to the selection.

I used Filter➡Stylize➡Find Edges for this result.

Filter➡Pixellate➡Crystallize applied in Step 4 gives us this rather subtle effect.

As another variation, skip Step 3 and eliminate feathering. Apply a filter to the inside area.

After a Gaussian Blur (15) the original image is recognizable only as the border.

That blurry rectangle seems like a great place for type. ▪

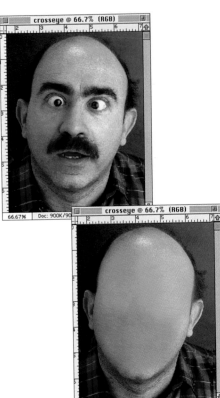

As a caricaturist I never met a face I didn't want to distort. Here's a fun drag-and-drop way to make faces.

**I** First we need a blank face. I started with the "Cross-eyed" guy from the Digital Stock folder on *Photoshop Effects Magic* CD-ROM. Use the Eyedropper tool to pick up face color and use a fat Airbrush to cover his features.

For the remaining steps you may use the ready-to-drag face parts in the ArtStart folder on the CD-ROM. Any other source images are fine.

34

**2** Drag and drop some features onto this blank expression.

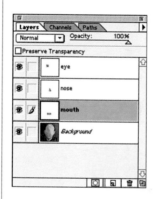

Each feature will have its own layer. Double-click a layer name and type in a descriptive label to avoid confusion.

**3** Use Layer➥Transform commands to alter size and position of the face parts. Try several combinations. I covered one mouth with another, enlarged the nose and flipped it horizontally, added another eye, and made the first eye invisible.

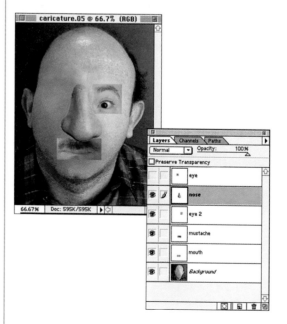

35

**4** Create a layer mask for each of the face parts that you want to blend into the background. Use the Airbrush tool and choose a foreground color of black, then spray gently around the edges of the added pieces. Because you're working on the layer mask, this will fade out the obvious edges, and if you make a mistake, switch the foreground color to white and repaint.

The Layers palette at this stage shows that the outer edges of both eyes and the nose have been masked out. The mustache layer mask is currently active, as you can see from the highlight color on the layer, the mask icon showing, and the black border around the layer mask.

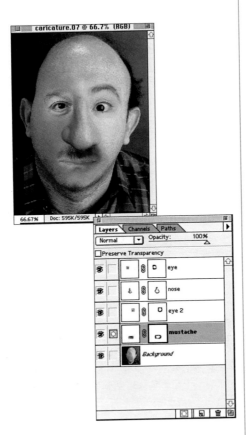

It's not realistic enough to fool anybody, and that's okay. To create more seamless face composites, read on.

# VARIATIONS

Suppose you want to combine expressions or facial features from two or more photographs realistically. You can do a seamless graft. All you need is the right donor.

**1** Open the images you want to work with. I'm using "Surprised" and "Delighted," in the Digital Stock folder on the CD-ROM.

**2** Double-click the Lasso tool to open the Lasso Options palette and set the feathering to 12. Draw a selection around the "Surprised" mouth with the Lasso tool, including a generous amount of extra skin.

**3** Drag and drop the donor mouth onto the recipient image. A new layer (Layer 1) for the mouth is created automatically.

37

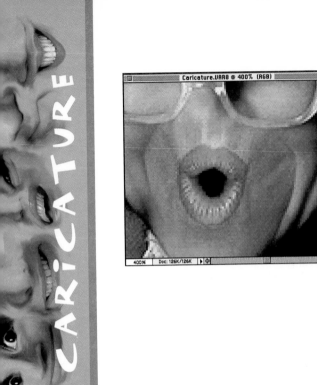

**4** Make sure Layer 1 is active and select Layer➧Transform➧Scale. Drag a corner handle of the bounding box to adjust the size of the new mouth. Press (Return)[Enter] to accept the change.

**5** Create a layer mask for the mouth layer. Now you can eliminate unwanted facial pixels safely.

**6** Choose a foreground color of black. With the Airbrush at low pressure (I used 16%) gently stroke away enough to reveal the nose in the background image. If you remove too much, switch to white and paint the pixels back in.

**7** I now saw that the new mouth wasn't lined up correctly with the recipient nose. I used Layer➧Transform➧Rotate and turned the mouth layer a few degrees counterclockwise. Press (Return)[Enter] to accept changes.

**8** Flatten the image and you're done.

## Tweaking and Tuning

You may want to do one or more of the following after the layers are merged.

I used a circular selection and applied the pinch filter (30%) to make the mouth a bit smaller. The grid in the Pinch preview box shows that the shrinking effect is applied gradually and is strongest in the center of the selection.

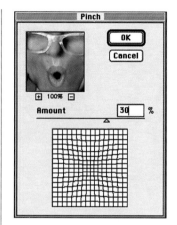

I tried to smooth away any remaining signs of the surgery. I used the Blur tool at 100% pressure to soften and blend some tell-tale edges but then, some of the skin around the mouth looked too smooth! I threw a feathered Lasso around these areas and used Filter➡Noise➡Add Noise (7, Uniform) to re-establish skin texture quickly.

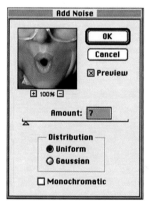

39

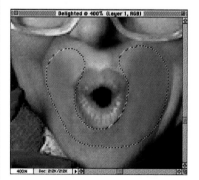

Another way to create quick caricature in Photoshop is with a few
simple distortions. Here's an image
called "Redhead" in the Digital
Stock folder of your CD-ROM.

1 Select➡All and use Layer➡
Transform➡Perspective to make
the head bigger in proportion to
the body, like this. When you pull
one of the corner handles out
(or in) the adjacent handle moves
automatically to create perspective.
It may take a moment for you to
get a feel for manipulating the handles to get the effect you want.

**2** Now you'll prepare to apply a distortion filter to her head. Use the elliptical Marquee and select the woman's face and hair. Select➠Feather (12 pixels).

**3** Apply Filter➠Distort➠Spherize (100%, Normal).

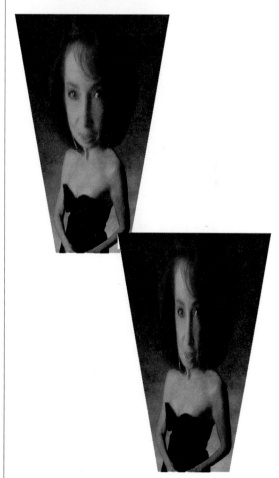

In Step 3, use Vertical only Mode instead of Normal, and you get something like this. Just imagine what you can do with photos of your family! ■

41

This technique shows how to create color by changing the relative positions of some of the pixels in each of the RGB channels.

If you have grayscale source images, but you're creating a color document, here's a great way to add vibrant color accents. You can shift an entire channel a few pixels for a neon glow, but be careful! Tell your prepress professional what you have in mind so she doesn't try to "fix" the registration for you.

1 Open the image you want to manipulate. I used "Earring" in the ArtStart folder on the *Photoshop Effects Magic* CD-ROM. Convert to RGB mode and save the image. I am going to select the earring and manipulate it differently in each channel.

Steps 2 through 7 show how to make an exact selection of the earring. Keep the Paths palette open for this sequence.

2 Choose the Pen tool and click the outside left edge of the earring. Then drag down and left.

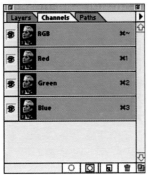

**3** Make your second click on the opposite side of the earring. This time, drag up and to the right.

**4** Close the shape by clicking the first point. You have just created a path using Bézier curves. Don't worry if your curve doesn't match the contour of the earring exactly.

**5** Choose the Direct Selection tool, in the Pen tool group. Use it to match the shape of the earring by moving anchor points or changing the length and angle of direction lines. This might take a few tries.

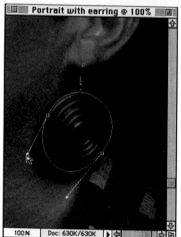

**6** Use the Save Path command in the Paths palette's arrow menu and then choose Make Selection. Name the path "earring," and turn off the path.

43

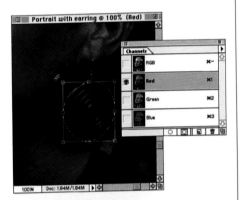

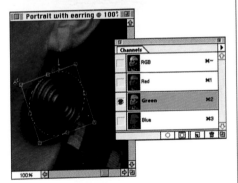

**TIP** If you've got a steady hand, you might prefer to select the earring with the Lasso tool and make adjustments as follows. To add to the selection, hold the Shift key down while dragging the Lasso around the pixels you missed. To subtract from the selection, hold down the (Command)[Control] key while you lasso the unwanted areas.

**7** Switch to default colors. Make the Red channel active and choose Layer➤Transform➤Rotate. The selection will have a bounding box. Drag one of the corner handles a few degrees clockwise. This rotates the selection in the Red channel only.

**8** Repeat Step 7 for the Green channel, but use a counterclockwise rotation. You don't need to change any pixels in the Blue channel.

Return to the composite channel to see your results. I created a neon color glow to the earring by offsetting pixels in each channel. The effect will be dramatic or subtle depending on the amount of offset or the techniques used to make changes.

**9** I cleaned things up by eliminating the neon "spill" on the edges with the Eraser tool set at Erase to Saved.

# VARIATIONS

You can start with a color image instead of grayscale. Using a color image gives you a wider range of color combinations when you off-set pixels. Try this with "Gold Beetle" in the Image Club folder on the book's CD-ROM.

**1** Using the Elliptical Marquee tool, select an oval area on the beetle's body. Feather the selection (12 pixels).

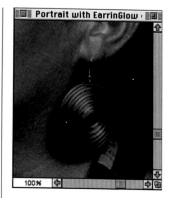

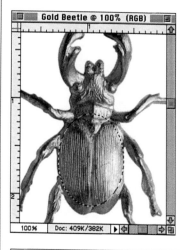

**2** Make the Red channel active. Use Layer➧Transform➧Numeric Transform and type in 90% for both vertical and horizontal scaling.

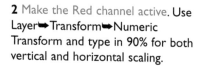

45

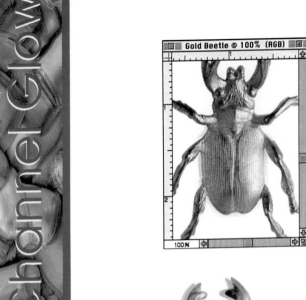

Gold Beetle @ 100% (RGB)

100%

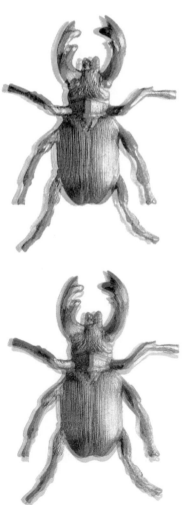

**3** Make the Green channel active. Repeat the Numeric Transform using 110%.

The composite image has an iridescent quality. You can eliminate the pinkish halo with the Erase to Saved function of the Eraser tool.

If that effect is too subtle, you can offset an entire channel rather than just a small element.

**1** Select➡All. Make the Red channel active.

**2** Hold down the (Command) [Control] key while clicking keyboard arrows. I moved the Red channel about 10 pixels to the left. Return to the composite channel to see your results.

**3** Repeat Step 2 for one of the other channels. I moved the Blue channel about 10 pixels down to produce this glowing beetle.

Another way to offset pixels is to apply different filter effects to each channel.

I opened the grayscale image called "Mask" from the Image Club folder on the CD-ROM. This time I converted to CMYK mode so I'd have an extra channel to play with.

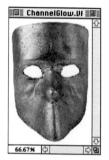

Here are the filter effects I applied to each channel:

Cyan: Artistic➡Fresco

Magenta: Artistic➡Poster Edges.

Yellow: Brush Strokes➡Dark Strokes

Black: no change ■

47

The Render➡Clouds filter can produce all kinds of weather, depending on your choice of colors and apply modes. Thanks to Patrick Lichty's excellent atmosphere effects for encouraging us to reach for the sky.

1 Open the image to which you would like to add clouds. I used "Brownstone," which is in the Digital Stock➡Urban Textures folder of your *Photoshop Effects Magic* CD-ROM.

2 Select the background building. I used the Lasso tool while holding down the (Option)[Alt] key. This enabled me to make straight line segments with clicks as I traced the left edge of the Brownstone building. Click the lower-left and the upper-right corner, then click your starting point to complete the selection. Press the Delete key to delete the background; keep the selection active.

**TIP** If you save the selection now, you can avoid having to repeat Step 2 if you lose the selection. Load the selection if you accidentally deselect the area in which you are creating the clouds.

**3** Switch to default colors. Select Filter➡Render➡Clouds to fill the background with gray cloud formations. Due to the random nature of the Clouds filter, repeat it until you like the results.

**TIP** **Use (Command-F) [Control-F] to reapply the Filter.**

To see your image without the "marching ants" use View➡Hide Edges (Command-H)[Control-H].

**4** I noticed a rim of pixels around the building that should have been deleted. That's easy to fix. I used Select➡Modify➡Expand (2 pixels). My next fill fit snugly against the building.

49

# VARIATIONS

**You need to** choose the foreground and background colors **to make** clouds before you apply the filter. Use blue instead of black for a sunny sky. I chose CMYK values of 47, 21, 0, 0 for this Cloud fill. With the selection still active, I used Image➡Adjust Brightness/Contrast and set Brightness to +14.

To create a smokey look, do the following after Step 3. First, be sure the sky is selected. Choose a foreground color of blue and choose a background color of white, and then apply another cloud fill over the black-and-white one. Access the fade control near the top of the Filter menu. Don't fade the effect, just choose Overlay mode, and you get something like this.

This threatening alien sky was made by choosing the foreground color red (0, 86, 73, 0) and choosing the background color purple (85, 94, 0, 0). The building would look pinker in this setting, wouldn't it? I selected the building, using the Select➡Inverse command. Then I used Edit➡Fill (20–30%) in Color mode to retain the contrast and detail.

To simulate fog, decrease the contrast and detail. After Step 3, deselect the sky and apply Clouds to the entire image. Now select Filter➡Fade. I faded the effect to 85%, and we might as well be in London…or San Francisco.  ■

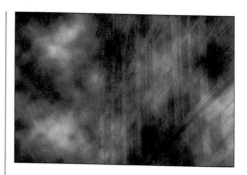

Collage is one of the most popular and effective uses for Photoshop. Image elements are put on separate layers, so they can be viewed in various combinations. Each item's size, position and opacity can be manipulated independently.

**I** Open the image you want to use as a background. I used "Postcards" from Image Club, which you can find in the Image Club folder on the *Photoshop Effects Magic* CD-ROM.

**2** Open the "Boots" image from the same folder.

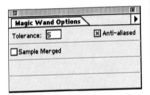

**3** Select the white area around the boots by clicking anywhere in it with the Magic Wand tool. If there are some unselected white pixels around the boots, increase the Tolerance in the Magic Wand Options palette. I used 5.

**4** Select➡Inverse selects the boot and not the background. That's what we had in mind all along.

**5** Drag and drop the boots to the "postcards" image. Boots automatically creates a new layer. Double-click "Layer 1" and rename it "Boots."

Repeat Steps 2 through 5 for the Baby Shoes and Brooch layers. It doesn't matter what position they are in temporarily, as long as they each occupy their own layer. As you did for the Boots layer, rename them descriptively to avoid confusion.

**6** Hide the Brooch layer and make the Baby Shoes layer active. Use the Move tool to drag the baby shoes down to the foreground of the image.

**53**

**7** Choose Layer➡Transform➡Flip Horizontal to make the baby shoes face the same direction as the boots. Select Layer➡Transform➡ Scale to reduce the size of the baby shoes to about half, or until they look proportional to the adult boots.

**8** Make the Boots layer active. Move the image to the left and slightly down

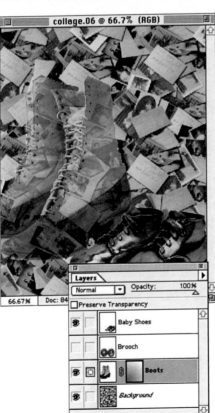

**9** Create a layer mask for the boots. Use the settings shown here to blend the boots into the background.

I experimented with several blending modes for the bronze Baby Shoes layer, finally deciding on Hard Light at 100% opacity.

I also wanted to fade them a bit on the left. Here's how:

**10** Create a layer mask for the baby shoes.

**11** Use the Airbrush tool at low pressure (I used 14%) to gently "black-out" some of the shoe. I've hidden all the other layers so you can see only the baby shoes.

Remember the brooch? We haven't seen it since Step 6. Make the Brooch layer active and hide the Background layer and the Baby Shoes layer. This makes it easier to concentrate on the relationship between the brooch and the boots.

**12** Choose Layer➡Free Transform to resize and rotate the image as shown.

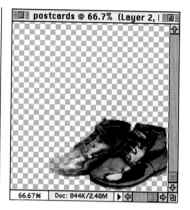

**13** Select Layer➡Transform➡ Distort to apply some perspective to the brooch.

**TIP** The Distort command enables you to move each corner handle independently, giving you more control than the Perspective command.

Make all the layers visible to see how the elements fit together. I'd still like to fade the brooch into the boot but everything else looks good.

**14** Double-click the Eraser tool and use Airbrush mode at 50% pressure. Gently brush out enough of the brooch so it blends into the boot. I thought I was close enough to completion that I didn't have to worry about changing my mind, so I didn't use a Layer Mask to produce this little fade.

**15** Drag each Layer Mask to the Trash icon on the Layers palette. You'll be asked if you want to Apply it or delete it. Choose Apply.

**TIP** It's a good idea to save a version in Photoshop format with all the layers and masks intact, just in case you or your client wants a last-minute change.

# Variations

There are many variations possible simply by changing the blending mode of the layers before you flatten them.

We start by altering the background.

**I** Make the Background layer active. (Command-I)[Control-I] inverts the color of the image. I faded the inversion to 75%.

**2** This new background suggested changes for the other collage items. I used Normal mode at 60% opacity for the Baby Shoes layer, Hard Light mode at 80% for the Brooch layer, and Multiply mode at 100% for the Boots layer.

Here's a version with the Baby Shoes layer in Luminosity mode and the Brooch layer in Color Burn mode. The boots have their colors inverted and use Difference mode. All layers are at 100% opacity.

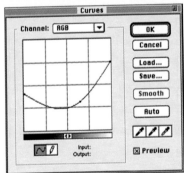

For the next variation, Gaussian Blur (radius: 15 pixels) is applied to the background, and the Fade command is used to change the mode to Lighten. The brooch has a color inversion and Exclusion mode. I altered the Boots layer with Image➡Adjust➡Curves and switched to Multiply mode.

The baby shoes have Filter➡
Artistic➡Plastic Wrap applied. Fade
the effect to 60% and change the
mode to Exclusion.  ■

The displacement maps might be hard to find at first, but once you have found them never let them go. These enchanted effects look like they took an entire evening to create, but all you need is a filter, a little fade, and your choice of blending mode.

It's easy to create a displacement map. It's a bit tougher to predict how they will behave. Any image in Photoshop format can function as a displacement map. An RGB image uses only the red and green channels to determine displacement. Essentially, the map influences how pixels in the target image will be distorted, based on color values. You can create a displacement map to produce a specific effect, once you get the hang of it, or just experiment.

1 Open the image you want to work with. I'm using "Smoker," in the Digital Stock folder on the *Photoshop Effects Magic* CD-ROM.

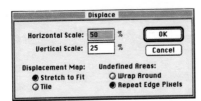

2 Select Filter➡Distort➡ Displacement. I used 50% horizontal and 25% vertical, for no particular reason, accepting the other default settings.

**3** Click OK and you'll be prompted to choose a displacement map. Navigate through your Photoshop folders to find them in the Plug-ins folder [dispmaps folder for Windows]. I chose Twirl.

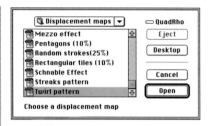

Here's the twirl displacement map.

And this is the effect it has on our smoker.

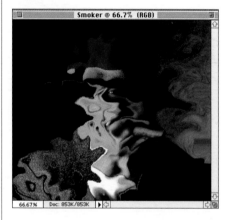

**4** Select Filter➡Fade (50%). In Normal mode, the 50% fade gives us equal parts of the original and the distorted image.

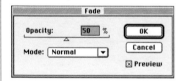

61

Switching to Exclusion mode makes for some excellent cigar smoke.

**5** If you're going for realism, get rid of those lumpy shapes on the left of his hat with the Eraser tool in "Erase to Saved" mode.

> **TIP** To repeat the last filter, use **(Command-F)[Control-F]** To change the settings for the last filter, use **(Option-Command-F)[Alt-Control-F]** and to fade last filter, use **(Shift-Command-F)[Shift-Control-F]**.

## VARIATIONS

If realism leaves you cold, displacement maps are your friends. Here's "Smiling Woman" and what I did to her with the Crumbles displacement map (50% vertical and 50% horizontal).

I faded the displacement to 70% and switched to Difference mode, getting this result.

The colors are great. The shapes and movement are an exciting surprise, but I wanted to soften some of the blotches on her skin and hair. I used the Rubber Stamp tool with the Impressionist option and one of the bristle brushes. See "Cloning" (page 96) and "Bristle Brush" (page 172) for details on this.

In the process of playing with displacement maps I began to create some visual references to keep track of combinations that seemed promising. Here are some of them.

Starting with a miniature version of PhotoDisc's Apple, this is Random Strokes (15% ).

This is the Streaks Pattern (15% for both horizontal and vertical).

Here's the result of using the map called "Twirl pattern" at 40% in Darken mode.

This candy comes from PhotoDisc, too.

Here's the candy using the Crumbly displacement map (15%) in Multiply mode.

I used the Mezzotint map at 15% in Lighten mode for this variation.

Finally, here's an eye chart you're not likely to find in a doctor's office. 10% displacement was applied to each of these. From left to right: Pentagons, Rectangular Tiles, Honeycomb.

There are a few custom displacement maps included in the Presets folder on your CD-ROM. ■

Here are some great techniques for adding a wet or glistening quality to a photographic image. They all involve using the Chrome filter and a choice of blending mode.

**1** Open the image you'd like to "juice up." I'm using "Orange" in the PhotoDisc folder on the *Photoshop Effects Magic* CD-ROM.

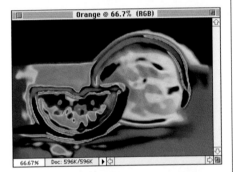

**2** Apply Filter➡Sketch➡ Chrome. The Chrome filter creates a gray-scale image that may make the original nearly unrecognizable. It may make an image look chrome-plated. But if you bring back some color, it's as if a thick layer of shiny goo has been poured over the image. The next step will bring back color.

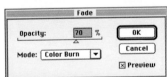

**3** Use Filter➡Fade to change the blending mode to Color Burn. I also faded the effect to 70%.

The Orange slice looks luscious and juicy, but I want to eliminate some of the reddish blotches on the orange rind.

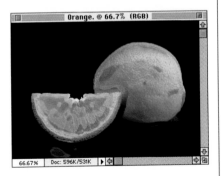

**4** Double-click the Eraser tool and check Erase to Saved. I used the Airbrush type and lowered opacity to have better control. I gently stroked in the original skin of the orange and some of the foreground. I cropped the photo to focus even more on that mouthwatering slice.

# VARIATIONS

This candy, also from PhotoDisc, looks yummy without any special effects. But it's tempting to try.

After applying the Chrome filter I used Filter➡Fade to change the blending mode to Soft Light (100%). This will melt in your mouth and in your hand.

© Copyright 1997 PhotoDisc, Inc.

Not only can you use this technique to make things look more delicious, but you can make them look more disgusting! Here's "Octopus" from PhotoDisc.

This is the slimy green thing I got after applying the Chrome filter and switching to Difference mode in the Filter➡Fade dialog box. Blecchhh.  ■

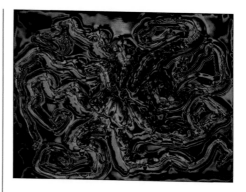

You can change shades of gray to shades of the foreground color by painting in Color mode. This technique shows how to create the look of handpainted crockery. Color mode is also used to imitate hand-tinted photographs on page 74.

**1** Open the image "Fruit Tea Pot grays." You can find it in the Image Club folder on the *Photoshop Effects Magic* CD-ROM.

**2** Convert the image to RGB mode. The image looks the same, but now it is a 3-channel image, and it is ready to accept color.

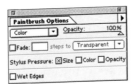

**3** Double-click the Paintbrush tool to open the Paintbrush Options palette and change from Normal mode to Color. I used 100% opacity. To imitate the strokes made by conventional brushes, turn Wet Edges on. This will produce a slight pooling of pigment on the edges of each stroke.

**4** Select a brush size big enough to fill an area with the minimum number of strokes and small enough to give you control. Use CMYK values 67, 59, 15, 17 for purple.

**5** Paint the grapes on both sides of the teapot. Your image should look something like this

Repeat Steps 4 and 5 for the apple. I used CMYK values of 25, 77, 69, 11.

**6** The apple looked too saturated (the color is too strong) in spots, so I used the Sponge tool in desaturate mode (23%) to absorb excess color.

This took out too much color, so I switched to saturate mode (11%) to paint some back in.

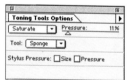

I colored the pear with CMYK values 19, 31, 87, 6. Again I chose to desaturate some of the lighter areas with the Sponge tool.

71

**7** The strawberries were a bit more involved. They appear to be painted with red and touches of yellow. I used the same red that I used for the apple, and added some strokes of the same yellow used on the pear. Now the image looks like this:

> **TIP** **When altering hue in Color mode, it's not necessary to remove the original color. There is no "buildup." Just paint over an area as often as you want. The transparency remains the same.**

Continue colorizing all parts of the teapot, touching up as needed with the Sponge.

Paint the leaves using these CMYK values 51, 27, 65, 25.

Brown CYMK Values 38, 45, 67, 29 are recommended for the handles and spout.

I used a light tan for the teapot with CYMK values 20, 20, 29, 1. That turnip or whatever it is to the upper-left of the apple is nearly the same color, with a bit of yellow added at low opacity.

You are finished. Now boil some water and sit back with a relaxing cup of tea. ◼

Before the popularity of color photography, artists were employed to apply color to sepia-tone or grayscale photos. Skin tone, eye color, rosy cheeks, and so on were added by hand with transparent pigment. This can be an effective way to imitate a retro look. A quick way to create transparent color is with the Fill command in Color mode.

A similar technique for hand-painted china is on page 70. In that one you want your brush strokes to show. In this one you don't.

**1** Open the grayscale image "typist" in the PhotoDisc folder on the *Photoshop Effects Magic* CD-ROM. Convert to RGB mode so it can accept color.

© Copyright 1997 PhotoDisc, Inc.

**2** Select➡All. Choose a foreground color with these CMYK values: 44, 48, 63, 37 and select Edit➡Fill. Use these settings in the Fill dialog box to create a sepia tone. Save the image.

**3** Double-click the Lasso tool and type in a feather value in the Options palette. I used 4. Draw around the woman's dress with the Lasso. Don't worry about getting your selection precise. Slight imperfections add charm.

**4** Choose a foreground color for the dress. I used CMYK values of 70, 29, 40, 27 and filled the selection at 50% opacity.

**5** Repeat Steps 4 and 5 for the hair. I used CMYK values of 11, 48, 49, 1 at 40% to give the hair an auburn tone.

**6** I switched to the Paintbrush in Color mode and used the same foreground color for the skin (40%) and lips (100%). Zoom in to control the application of lipstick. If you get lipstick on her teeth, use the Erase To Saved function of the Eraser Tool for a touch-up.

**7** Finally, use the Airbrush tool to apply blush to her cheeks. I set the opacity at 3%. ■

When is a lighting effect not a lighting effect? When it's a transparent gradient!

The Transparent Stripes preset is put through its paces in my "Kaleidoscope" technique (page 194). Here I used it to make a variety of checkerboard patterns.

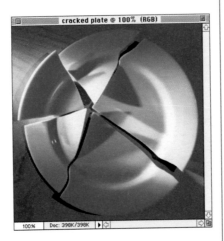

**1** Open the image you want to work with. I started with a photograph that already has some exciting lighting. It's "Plate" from the PhotoDisc folder on the *Photoshop Effects Magic* CD-ROM.

**2** Create a new layer (Layer 1).

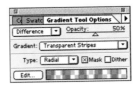

**3** Double-click the Gradient tool and use these settings. The foreground color I'm using is burnt sienna (CMYK values 24, 89, 100, 11).

**4** With Layer 1 still active, drag the Gradient tool from the upper-left corner of the image to the lower-right corner.

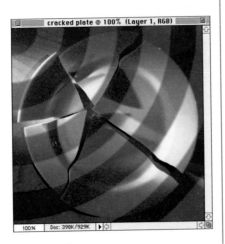

**5** With the same gradient settings, drag another diagonal from the lower-left to the upper-right of the image.

**6** Switch the blending mode in the Layers palette to Difference. There's your "blue plate special."

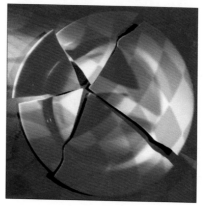

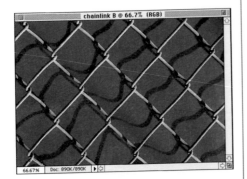

chainlink B @ 66.7% (RGB)

66.67%  Doc: 890K/890K

## VARIATIONS

This chainlink image from Digital Stock's Urban Textures collection inspired another diamond design. You'll find this photo in the Urb/Tex file on the CD-ROM.

I switched the gradient type to Linear, leaving the blending mode on Difference and the Opacity at about 50% as before. My foreground color was olive green (CMYK 51, 22, 79, 17) for the first diagonal drag and mustard yellow (CMYK 25, 11, 97, 20) for the second drag.

Here's how Layer 1 looks with the background image invisible.

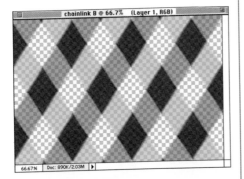

chainlink B @ 66.7%  (Layer 1, RGB)

66.67%  Doc: 890K/2.03M

The composite image, with Layer 1 in Difference mode, looks like a patterned fabric has been placed behind the fence.

This tablecloth for an Italian restaurant doesn't require a photo or an additional layer. I created a new white square and used Red at 50% for each diagonal. Gradient type was linear and blending mode was Normal. ■

You can imitate some of the old masterpieces of the Impressionist or Post-Impressionist school by turning a photo into a glorious painting. I recommend using a pressure-sensitive tablet if you have one.

**1** Open the image you want to work with. I'm using "Fruit" in the PhotoDisc folder on the *Photoshop Effects Magic* CD-ROM. Fill the selection with background color medium gray. I used CMYK values 45, 32, 31, 9.

Those realistic colors will have to go. Black shadows? I don't think so.

© Copyright 1997 PhotoDisc, Inc.

**2** Apply the Yellow-Orange-Yellow Gradient using these settings. Drag vertically from top to bottom (or the reverse).

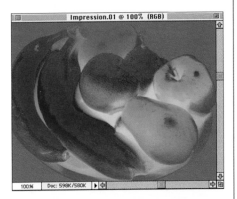

**3** Select Image➡Adjust➡Invert to get something like this:

82

**4** Load the Assorted Brushes. I've indicated my favorites for adding brush strokes and texture. Do most of your "painting" with the Smudge tool at 100% and one or more assorted brush tips.

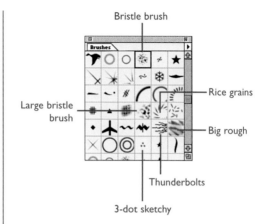

Bristle brush

Large bristle brush

Rice grains

Big rough

Thunderbolts

3-dot sketchy

**5** Use a variety of strokes to smudge out detail and blend edges. Strokes that follow the contours of the shapes are most effective.

> **TIP** Long scribbly strokes are **fun, but they may take a while to appear. If you hate waiting as much as I do, try shorter strokes.**

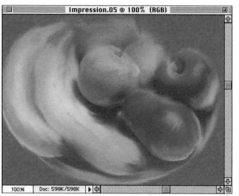

Impression.05 @ 100% (RGB)

100%   Doc: 598K/598K

**6** Add a more painterly background by sampling colors from the image with the Eyedropper and using low or medium opacity paintbrush strokes. I used the "Rice-grains" brush to add color and "Thunderbolts" to blend it with the Smudge tool.

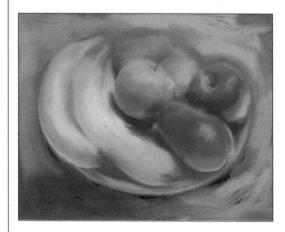

83

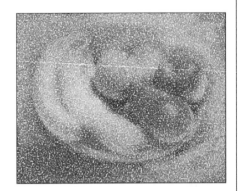

## VARIATIONS

Admirers of George Seurat may continue, adding a Pointillist effect. Apply Filter➥Pixellate➥Pointillize (Cell size: 3).

To get finer dots and no white spots, use the Add Noise Filter to create the Pointillist effect. I used these settings and then the Fade command to reduce the noise to about 60% in Dissolve mode.

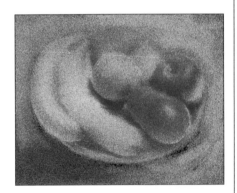

Fat, geometric dots enable you to jump ahead several decades to the Pop Art or Op Art style. After Step 6, apply Filter➡Pixelate➡Color Halftone. I used a Max. Radius of 6 and the default values for screen angles. ■

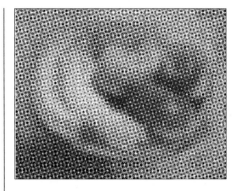

Photoshop 4.0 has a vast array of filters for applying traditional graphic effects. We'll layer and combine some of the effects from the Artistic category to create the look of pastel chalks.

Duplicating an image as additional layers is the first step to a wide variety of blend effects. See "Woodcut" on (page 116) for another example.

**1** Open the "Sourpuss" image in the Digital Stock folder on the *Photoshop Effects Magic* CD-ROM.

**2** Duplicate the layer. Name the layer "cutout." Apply Filter➡ Artistic➡Cutout, using these settings.

The portrait has been turned into a silkscreen print.

**3** Duplicate the background layer again. Name this third layer "pencil." Select Filter➡Artistic➡Colored Pencil. I used these values: Width 4, Pressure 8, Brightness 25. The pencil layer looks like this:

**4** You guessed it…duplicate the original layer again, and name it "Fresco." Apply Filter➡Artistic➡ Fresco. I accepted the default values for Size 2, Detail 8, and Texture 1. Here's the result.

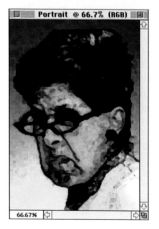

I reduced the opacity of the Fresco layer to 35%, and lowered the opacity of the pencil layer to 50%. Leaving the Cutout layer at 100% completely covers the original image, so I deleted the background layer.

## VARIATIONS

This time I used filters from the Sketch category.

Traditional artists often begin by laying out the areas of light and shadow, and adding details later. The Torn Edges filter gives you a black-and-white simplification of the forms. I softened the harsh black-and-white to light and dark gray by using Image➡Adjust➡Brightness/ Contrast (Brightness: +50, Contrast: -60).

I used the Conte Crayon filter for the detail layer. Here's how the combination looks with Conte Crayon in Multiply mode at 100% opacity. The canvas texture is a welcome addition.

I added one more layer and applied the Chrome filter, not a traditional look by itself.

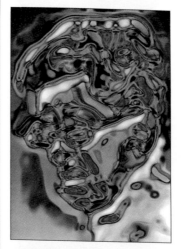

In combination with the other two layers and at 30% opacity, though, I got an interesting wet-on-wet character in some areas.

This kind of experimentation is finished whenever you say so. ∎

One of my favorite filters is "Pinch." It's great for distortion effects. And it's handy for making seamless gradual size reductions of a part of your image after you have merged layers.

I Open the image you want to pinch. Here I used the "Sourpuss" image, which is included in the Digital Stock folder on the book's CD-ROM. This lady looks like something is already pinching her.

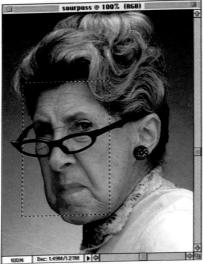

2 Use the rectangular Marquee selection tool and select the area you want to pinch. No feathering is needed, because the Pinch effect will fade out at the edges of the selection automatically.

**3** Apply Filter➡Distort➡Pinch. Notice the changes in the preview window as you drag the Amount slider. Increasing the percentage reduces the size of her features and brings them closer to the center of her face. I used 58%.

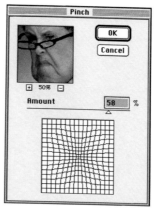

I know that woman! She was my faculty advisor in high school.

Notice the problem with her eyeglasses. They now appear to be in reverse perspective but that won't take long to fix.

To adjust the eyeglasses:

**1** Make a rectangular selection as shown.

sourpuss @ 100% (RGB)

100%    Doc: 597K/597K

**2** Use Layer➡Transform➡Distort and reshape the selection by dragging on the handles of the bounding box.

**3** Now patch up that white space with a gradient fill. Use the Eyedropper tool to pick up the foreground color from a brown pixel just above the white space. The background color should match the lighter brown just below the white space.

> **TIP** **Hold the Option key down when you want the Eyedropper to** choose a background color**.**

If you're a perfectionist, you may want to use the Add Noise filter to match the photo's graininess. This is close enough for one of those supermarket tabloids with a headline such as: "Woman eats 5-pound lemon and lives!"

sourpuss @ 100% (RGB)

100%    Doc: 597K/597K

# VARIATIONS

Open "Smiling Woman" in the Digital Stock folder on the book's CD-ROM.

The Pinch filter has a range that includes negative values. As you might expect, the larger the negative number, the more the selection bulges out. I applied a –42 Pinch to the mouth of the "Smiling Woman" with the selection off-center, resulting in a slightly lopsided smile.

You might as well polish her teeth while you're at it, using the Dodge tool (Midtones, 50% pressure).

Making her squint was accomplished with a circular selection and 100% pinch for each eye.

You can use a shortcut to duplicate the effect on the second eye: move the selection over and press (Command-F)[Control-F] to repeat the last filter.

The finishing touch was a long ellipse enclosing both eyes, and the Pinch filter at 35%. This brought the eyes slightly closer together.

93

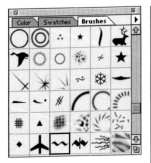

There are lots more uses for the pinch filter than just caricature.

Use it to create a crimp design for a pattern fill. I used the Brush shown, from the Assorted Brushes group.

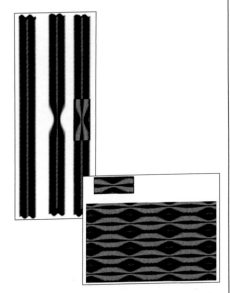

I made a straight stroke by holding the Shift key down as I painted. Then I selected and pinched a portion of the line a few times, colored it and flipped it 90 degrees. Then I used Edit➡Define Pattern followed by Edit➡Fill (Pattern) to pour this design into a new selection.

Pinch some type. Here's Benguiat Book in 36 points. I made a rectangular selection just fitting around the word and set the Pinch filter to 40.

I made the pinch more extreme by repeating the effect (Command-F) [Control-F].

Give type some punch with the Pinch filter in a negative value. Here's the same type with the Pinch value −55 ■

Pinch

Pinch

Punch

There are many ways of combining two or more images in Photoshop. See "Collage" (page 52) and "Blends" (page 22). This one is a favorite of mine because it is so direct and immediate. You don't need to use masks for this technique, but a tablet and stylus is recommended for complete control of the brush strokes.

The Rubber Stamp tool offers a powerful array of techniques for cloning images or parts of images into other images.

One exciting way to combine two photographs is to use one of them as the canvas and the other as the paintbrush. You need two photos for this recipe, one the source and the other the destination.

1 Open the two images you want to work with. I'm using "Clocks" and "SnuffBox" found in the Image Club folder on the *Photoshop Effects Magic* CD-ROM.

**2** Select a rectangular area on the snuffbox like this. Selecting Edit➡ Define Pattern makes the turquoise mosaic a source for the next step.

**3** Double-click the Rubber Stamp tool and choose the Pattern (non-aligned) option. Activate the Clock image and paint a few strokes over the clock faces. I used 50% opacity with a fairly fat brush and varied the blending modes. Some strokes use Normal mode, some use Difference mode. A few of the strokes were in Color Burn or Hard Light mode. Your image might look something like this.

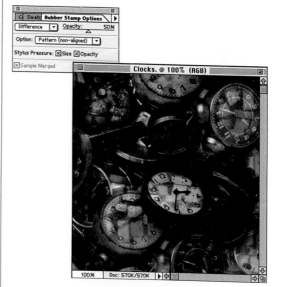

**4** You can add a painterly edge to the image. Be sure white is the background color, then select Image➡Canvas Size to add a white border about ¼-inch wide.

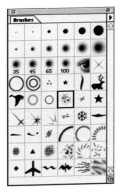

**5** Change to the Impressionist mode in the Rubber Stamp Options palette. Load Assorted Brushes if necessary and use the brush shown here. At 100% pressure and Normal mode, drag short strokes from inside the edges of the Clocks image into the white border.

Continue applying short, curved strokes here and there throughout the image. The effect is to reduce detail and create bristly brush strokes.

If you obliterate too much detail in spots, you can bring back the original pixels by switching to the From Saved option. This is very similar to the Erase to Saved option of the Eraser tool.

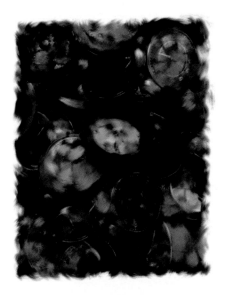

## VARIATIONS

This time Clocks is the source and SnuffBox will be altered with the Rubber Stamp tool.

**I** (Option-click)[Alt-click] the Clock image to establish the starting point for cloning.

**2** Activate the SnuffBox image and paint. I used Difference mode at about 60% and the Clone (non-aligned) option.

Try using "Teapot" as the source image. (It's in the Image Club folder on the book's CD-ROM.)

(Option-click)[Alt-click] the center of the teapot. Use Clone (aligned) this time.

For the background, select most of the teapot, excluding handle, spout, and cover. Edit➡Define Pattern and paint the background with one of the bristle brush tips. This one was done using Pattern (aligned) and Exclusion mode. ■

"Hand-Tinted" (page 70) shows how to add color to a grayscale image. Here you learn how to remove or minimize color, and add it back selectively to create emphasis.

**1** Open the image "IdaJello" in the ArtStart folder on the *Photoshop Effects Magic* CD-ROM.

**2** Select➡All. Select Image➡ Adjust➡Desaturate to remove all color in the image. Do not save, because you need to be able to restore part of the color image.

**3** Double-click the Eraser tool and select Erase to Saved in the Eraser Options palette. Use the settings shown here.

**4** Erase over the jello and fruit. This will bring back the color at full strength in the areas you stroke.

**5** I accidentally colored Ida's thumbs. No problem. If that happens to you, choose the Sponge tool. Select Desaturate mode at 100% pressure in the Toning Tools Options palette. Now paint over the areas you want to return to grayscale.

# VARIATIONS

You don't have to eliminate color completely. You can reduce the intensity of color to any level. Then "paint" back more intense color where you want it.

"Rooster" is a colorful image in Image Club➡Objects folder on the CD-ROM.

I used Image➡Adjust➡Hue/Saturation and moved the Saturation slider down to –65 to achieve this washed-out look.

Using the Erase to Saved function of the Eraser tool I brought back the color in the rooster's comb and wattles. ■

A traditional commercial art style that is becoming popular again is stippling—black-and-white art consisting of tiny dots. The old-fashioned way is tedious and time-consuming, one dot at a time, but with Photoshop it's a snap.

The method works best with photographs that have good contrast and lots of texture or detail. I'll use "Orange" from the PhotoDisc folder on the *Photoshop Effects Magic* CD-ROM.

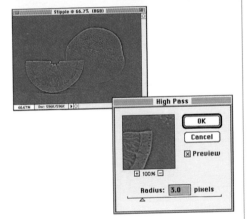

**I** Apply Filter➨Other➨High Pass to the entire image. This produces a medium gray except for the areas of greatest contrast. A low setting (1 to 3) is recommended. The lower the setting the stronger the effect.

**2** Use Image➨Adjust➨Threshold to turn the mostly gray image into black-and-white. Move the Threshold slider, or type the number you want. Most of the pixels are in the medium gray area, so small changes near the center of the threshold curve will produce large effects.

Here's the image with a threshold of 129. There is a great deal of black, especially in the background.

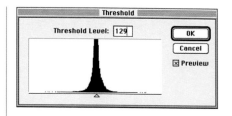

I reduced the threshold by only 2 pixels to get this change. Now most of the background pixels are white.

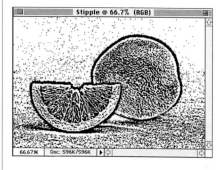

Move the threshold down to 120 and some of the detail is lost, but we can still identify the subject easily.

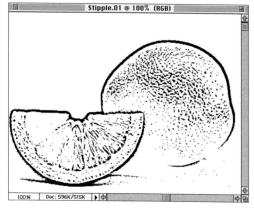

## VARIATIONS

We'll add color back to the lightly stippled orange.

1 Use the Save As command on your stippled image. Open the original photo again.

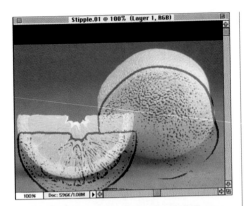

**2** Select➡All of the stippled version. Drag and drop it to the original color photo where it becomes Layer 1. Reduce opacity of Layer 1 so you can move it into position exactly over the color (background) layer.

Adjust the opacity of Layer 1 if needed to get a delicate watercolor wash effect. This is at 60%.

When your intention is to use the original photo as a color source, begin by using the Duplicate Layer command in the Layers palette menu. Then the stippling effect is applied to this "Background copy" layer. Of course, the two layers are perfectly aligned.

Sherry London's "Woodcut" was the inspiration for this recipe. You can find it on page 116. ■

A vignette is an image, usually small, which fades out at the edges. It's often used by conventional portrait photographers, but any subject is fair game. Here's a classic vignette.

**1** Open the file you want to vignette. I used the "Glamour" image in the Digital Stock folder on the *Photoshop Effects Magic* CD-ROM.

**2** Use the Elliptical Marquee tool and make an oval selection like this.

> **TIP** Hold down the (Option) [Alt] key and drag from the center for more control.

**3** Choose Selection➡Feather (16 pixels). The larger the number, the more gradual the fade-out will be.

**4** Select➡Inverse to select everything outside the oval.

**5** Press D to switch to default colors. Press the Delete key and the background fills with white, fading out toward the portrait.

Notice the upper part of the vignette has a hard edge. There wasn't enough space in the image above her hair to allow for the feathering. Let's start again and fix that problem.

**6** Choose File➡Revert to return to the original image.

**7** Choose Image➡Canvas Size and use the settings shown. Click OK and more space is added to the top of the image. It is white space, so fill it with black, using the Paint Bucket tool.

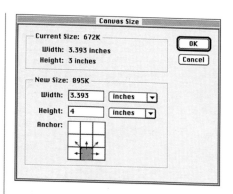

Repeat Steps 2 through 5. This time there is plenty of room at the top for a perfect vignette.

# VARIATIONS

A vignette can be any shape and fade to any color. These variations show some of the possibilities.

Use the "Toasting" image from the Digital Stock folder on the book's CD-ROM. Draw a selection with the Lasso tool, roughly corresponding to the group of figures, including the upraised glasses.

109

camelot (RGB, 1:1)

636K/636K

Do Steps 3 and 4, but choose a background color before you press the Delete key. I used CMYK values of 30, 87, 100, 29 for this reddish brown.

This variation uses a filter effect for a gradual fade to gray that allows some of the original image to remain.

You can find the "Camelot" image in the Digital Stock folder of the book's CD-ROM.

Make an oval selection of the queen's head. I used a large feather radius (45 pixels). Select➡Inverse to select everything except the queen's head. Apply Filter➡Other ➡High Pass to the selection, using a radius of 0.4 pixels. The High Pass filter reduces everything to medium gray except areas of high contrast.

This resulted in a fade-out where the filigree design on the King's jacket and some other lines remain visible.  ■

If you've ever wondered how to make fancy wallpaper out of fish heads look no further. You can crop an element from any complex image and make it into a tile for a repeating pattern.

**1** Open the file that contains the image you want on your wallpaper. I used "fish," which is in the Photo-Disc folder on the *Photoshop Effects Magic* CD-ROM. Make a rectangular selection as shown.

**2** Choose Edit➡Define Pattern to store the fish head as a pattern tile.

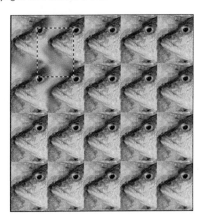

**3** Create a new file about 3 square inches to test the fish head pattern. Select Edit➡Fill and choose Pattern for Contents.

The fish heads do not form a seamless fill, and that's not surprising. It's easy to get a perfect pattern when the image element is "floating" in a solid color background. However, this technique requires a bit of trial-and-error.

**4** Select a new rectangle for a repeating tile, using the fish eyes as guides. Use the Smear tool to blend the area that showed the seam. Select Edit➥Define Pattern to replace the original fish head with this new tile and test it by using Edit➥Fill again.

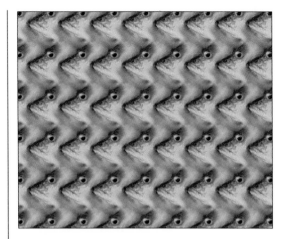

## VARIATIONS

Here's a striped wallpaper that was easy to make. The tile element is the same fish head we used in Step I and a chunk of beef (you can find "rawmeat" in the PhotoDisc folder on the CD-ROM).

It's not quite seamless, but the tiling doesn't intrude that much. I call it "Surf and Turf."

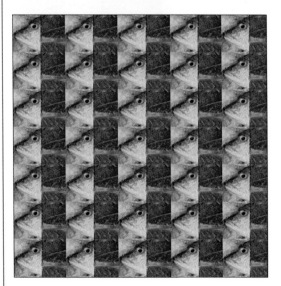

113

For the vegetarians, I recommend using the "Squash" image in the PhotoDisc folder on the CD-ROM. Select an area such as this one and copy it to the clipboard.

Paste it into a new file about 4 inches wide by 2.5 inches high. Paste again and choose Layer➡ Transform➡Flip Horizontally. Choose Layer➡Merge Layers.

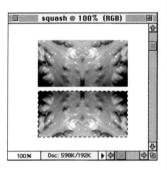

Copy the new double image and then flip it vertically. Move it into place to create a 4-way mirror image. Touch up any seams with the Smudge tool.

This image is the pattern tile for a more elaborate-looking fill. Crop it carefully before you use Edit➡ Define Pattern. Your fill may look something like this. ■

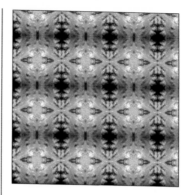

Sherry London's "Woodcut" technique is one of many ways to create effects beginning with two identical layers.

You can imitate the look of a woodblock print by changing the top layer into black-and-white detail and making the white areas transparent. This creates a bold, rough-textured graphic similar to traditional relief prints.

**1** Open the file you'd like to use. I am working with "Alphabet Blocks," which is in the Image Club folder on the *Photoshop Effects Magic* CD-ROM. The ideal image for this technique has a wide range of shapes, good contrast, and is not too dark.

**2** Duplicate the background layer. Steps 3 to 6 are applied to this "Background copy" layer.

**3** Apply Filter➡Other➡High Pass (2.5). The High Pass filter produces medium gray except in areas of highest contrast. The lower the value, the stronger the effect.

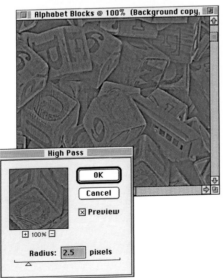

**4** Choosing Image➥Adjust➥ Desaturate will remove what little color remains. Your image should look something like this:

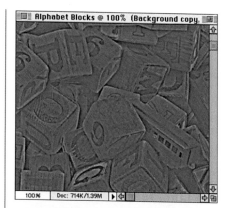

**5** Select Image➥Adjust➥Posterize (2). Using 2 levels makes all the pixels on this layer either black or white. Remember that we will make the white areas transparent.

**6** Switch the blending mode of the layer to Multiply. The white areas of the layer become transparent, so the original colors of the background can show through.

Here's the finished "block print" image.

## VARIATIONS

To get a wet-on-wet watercolor look in the color layer, do this last. Make the background layer active and apply Filter➡Blur➡Gaussian Blur (7 pixels).

You can control the ratio of white to black in Step 5 by using Image➡Adjust➡Threshold instead of Posterize.

If you want the look of sticky, heavily applied black ink, move the Threshold slider to the right to make more pixels black. Here's the complete image when I moved the Threshold right to 137.

Another adjustment or two and we'll get the look of a "crayon scratchboard" image.

**1** Flatten the image.

**2** Increase both Brightness and Contrast (I used +25).

**3** Select All and use Image➡ Adjust➡Hue/Saturation. I moved the Saturation slider up to 70 for hot color to show through the "scratches." ■

# PART II

## Using Line Art

Anything strictly black-and-white meets my definition of line art. So, that covers cartoons, lots of clip art and type. Even EPS or vector art can be manipulated in Photoshop. When you have placed such an item in a Photoshop document, it becomes a bit-map or raster image, and it can be manipulated with any of Photoshop's tools. I've also included the paths made with Photoshop's Pen tool in this category.

This section covers several ways for applying color to line art, distorting clip art, a couple of dandy Type effects, and a great way to prepare artwork for two-color printing. The two-color technique as well as Burning Type and Quick Color work much better if you are using a graphics tablet. Have I mentioned that it would be a good idea to get one?

Sharron Evans asks, "How do you apply color to a black-and-white drawing and not worry about covering up the black lines or filling in the open/white areas and then having to correct a white halo between the black lines and the color due to dithering or anti-aliased lines?" We've all asked ourselves that question from time to time, haven't we?

Sharron suggests managing your colorizing problems by creating a second layer for color and placing it under the black-and-white layer. Because nothing can go under the background this takes a few steps.

**1** Open your black-and-white line art. I'm using "Vrtual66" in the ArtStart folder on the *Photoshop Effects Magic* CD-ROM. Convert the image to RGB mode.

**2** Duplicate the Background layer. It will be called "Background copy" automatically.

**3** Create a new layer and name it "color." Drag the color layer below the Background copy layer in the Layers palette. Rename the Background copy layer "line art" to avoid confusion.

**4** The original Background layer is no longer needed, so delete it. Your Layers palette looks like this.

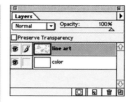

**5** Make the line art layer active and choose Darken in the blending mode menu. Darken mode will protect anything darker than the color you are using to paint with. Because black is the darkest possible color, you can paint without fear of harming any of the linework. Now make the color layer active.

> **TIP** **Keep the Swatches palette open for quick access to a reasonable variety of colors. You can add extra colors by choosing them in the color picker and clicking the empty area in the Swatches palette. To choose a background color from the Swatches palette, hold down the (Option) [Alt] key.**

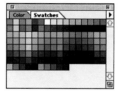

Painting large areas with flat color can get tedious. What about filling them with the paint bucket or gradient tool?

At this stage my color work includes the rider's hands and neck painted with a fleshtone, and the same color bucket fill for his face. I selected the computer and keyboard with several Magic Wand selections, holding down the Shift key, so they could be added together and filled with a single click. Some gaps still need to be painted in "by hand."

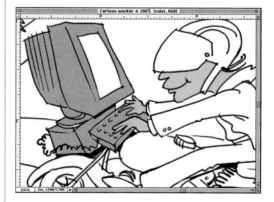

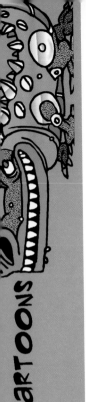

The following steps show how to manipulate selections efficiently and maneuver between layers.

**1** Make the line art layer active and use the Magic Wand to select the areas you want to fill.

**2** Adjust the pixel tolerance in the Magic Wand Options palette.

The default value for Magic Wand tolerance is 32. When I used that amount and clicked on the front fender, the selection included the front tire because of a small line gap. Rather than altering the line layer (and possibly spoiling the spontaneous quality of the cartoon) I deselected and lowered the tolerance to 5. Now the tire was not included in the selection.

**3** Shift-click all the areas you want to fill with the same color.

**4** Make the color layer active and the same areas will be selected.

**5** Use Edit➡Fill if you want to control opacity. Otherwise just click with the paint bucket in any part of a selection and all selections will be filled.

**6** Hide the "marching ants" (Command-H)[Control -H] so you can see how well the areas were filled.

Using a tolerance of 5 leaves a "halo" of pixels, but you don't have to go all the way back to Step 2 to fix that. You don't even have to undo the fill if it was 100% opacity.

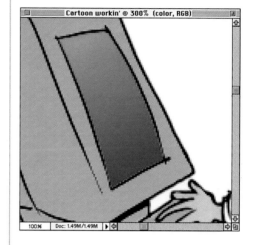

**7** Choose Select➡Modify➡Expand to increase the selection border by one or two pixels and repeat the fill. You still may need to touch up some edges with the paintbrush.

A gradient fill of the cartoon computer screen shows a "halo" at 300% magnification.

Expanding the selection area and redoing the fill solves the problem.

**8** Select the grass in the foreground with the Magic Wand tool at a tolerance of 5. It's hard to tell what's included, so do a test fill. Remember to make the color layer active before you use the Paint Bucket. I used a yellow-green with CMYK values 32, 0, 76, 0. The pine tree and the distant mountains are filled but the building is untouched.

**9** Use the Lasso tool to subtract the mountains from the selection. Hold down the (Option)[Alt] key and drag a closed loop around the area you want to deselect. I decided to use a gradient fill using a darker green (CMYK 75, 0, 100, 0) for the background color, dragging from the bottom to the top of the selection.

At some point it may be more efficient simply to merge layers and use Darken mode for the painting and filling tools, like when you keep forgetting to switch layers (as I do), or you become confident enough in your skills to rely on Erase to Saved as your safety net. See "Quick Color" (page 154) for some pointers on painting with Darken mode.

## Filling with Patterns

I used a pattern fill for the snazzy fabric on his suit.

**1** Open a postscript pattern. This is Herringbone 1.

**2** Select➡All and use the Edit➡ Define Pattern command.

**3** Select the areas of the cartoon you want to fill with the pattern. Edit➡Fill and use Pattern for Contents. I reduced opacity to 50%. To color the pattern, choose a foreground color then apply Edit➡Fill to the same selection at 25% opacity.

127

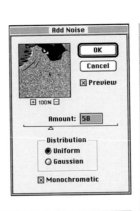

The asphalt highway was a combination of gradients and the Add Noise filter with these settings.

Some glaring gaps remain after the roadway was paved.

Repair them with the Rubber Stamp tool in Darken mode.

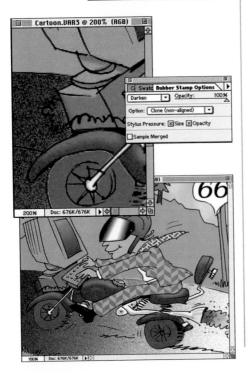

Well, this turned into quite a project, involving a lot more Photoshop skills than meet the eye. After some airbrush work on the tires, a few tiny eraser strokes to show off the wheel spokes…hmm, what if we showed reflections of the environment on his helmet visor? ■

2-color art

Graphic designers and illustrators can get plenty of mileage from this technique. It shows how to create an image for two-color printing. No, we're not talkin' duotones; that's something completely different.

This method involves working in CMYK and making the contents of two of the color channels disappear. Make sure you discuss this with your prepress person, who may have some additional guidelines.

**1** Create a new file (grayscale, 200 dpi).

**2** Paste or place any line art you want to work with. I'm using the EPS images "Cupcake" and Cake," which you'll find in Image Club➡ Sketches on the *Photoshop Effects Magic* CD-ROM. Each item creates its own layer. Use the Layer➡ Transform commands and the Move tool to arrange and size them like this. You'll have to erase a bit of the cake plate that shows through the cupcake frosting.

**3** Flatten the image. Convert to CMYK mode.

Let's say some shade of red will be used as the second color for printing. The exact color doesn't matter. We'll work in the Magenta channel because it is the one most similar to red and will give us the best visual approximation to the final printed piece.

**4** Make the Yellow channel active. Select➡All and delete. Repeat this with the Cyan channel.

**5** Make the Black channel active and make the composite channel visible. Your channels palette should look something like this.

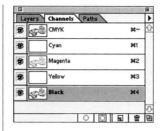

**6** With the Eraser tool, remove all the areas you want to print in shades of red. You can select areas and delete them or fill them with white, or paint them with white; whatever it takes to get rid of them. Here's how mine looks at this stage:

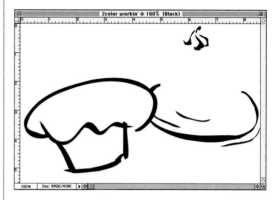

> **TIP** If you want to see each channel in the appropriate color instead of grayscale go to File➥Preferences➥ Display and Cursors. Check the Color Channels in Color checkbox.

**7** Make the Magenta channel active and erase everything you want to print in black or shades of gray. You may prefer to have the Black channel invisible so you can see more clearly what is being eliminated.

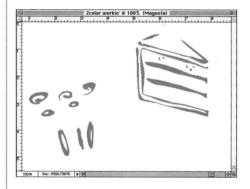

> **TIP** Print a screenshot of each channel for a good look at stray pixels that escaped your notice. My Magenta and Black channels both show some stray pixels to be eliminated.

To create different percentages of color in either channel, use shades of gray to paint or fill any area.

**8** In the Black channel I selected the "body" of the cupcake with a click of the Magic Wand. Then I used the Edit➡Fill command and chose 50% gray for the content.

**9** With both channels visible and the Magenta channel active, I made a freehand selection of the cupcake frosting with the Lasso tool. I feathered it (12) and used the 50% gray fill to get pink frosting.

**10** With Magenta still the target channel, I selected the area of the cake slice inside the frosting and used Edit➡Fill with 50% gray at 50% opacity to get a 25% shade of pink.

**TIP** Use the Lasso tool's polygon function to make the selection. Hold down the (Option)[Alt] key while you click corner points.

## VARIATIONS

You can start with a blank CMYK file. I made the Cyan channel active and chose a foreground color of medium gray. Filter➡Render➡ Clouds produced this blue sky.

With the composite channel active, place some EPS clip art and it goes to the black channel automatically. I'm using "Bird" from the Image Club➥Woodcuts folder on the book's CD-ROM.

With the Black channel active, I selected the white areas of the bird with the Magic Wand. Switching to the Cyan channel, I painted over the bird with rapid strokes and small brushes. Here's what the Cyan channel looked like with the Black channel invisible.

Say you want to use two "spot" colors in addition to basic black. I added the EPS image "Butterfly" and colored it in the Magenta channel. I kept the Black channel visible to use as a guide, but I didn't make any selections. Here's the Magenta channel, showing a variety of shades.

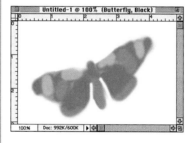

Here's the Final Image. ■

133

Use any font you want to try this technique for setting fire to type. I've included the text "Hot Coffee" in the ArtStart folder on the *Photoshop Effects Magic* CD-ROM. Appropriately enough, this effect makes excellent use of the Color Burn blending mode!

**1** Create a new file the appropriate size for your type. Fill it with golden yellow (CMYK: 11, 29, 90, 2).

**2** Enter the text in a rich brown (CMYK: 37, 69, 53, 56). Move the type to the lower part of the image, leaving plenty of room at the top for smoke and flames. Flatten the image.

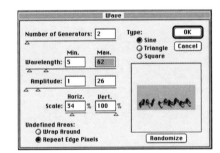

**3** Apply Filter➡Distort➡Wave. Fiddle with the numbers and sliders and radio buttons in the Wave dialog box until you like what you see in the preview. Even if you copy these settings you can get more choices by clicking the Randomize button.

 134

**4** Duplicate the Background layer. Switch the blending mode to Color Burn at 100% opacity.

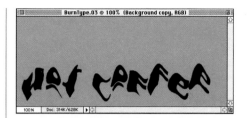

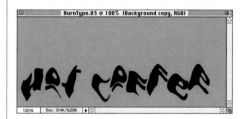

**5** Load Assorted Brushes. Use the "thunderbolt" Brush tip with the Smudge tool to drag smoky streaks through the type on the background layer.

With the Background copy invisible, the Background layer should look something like this during the smudging process.

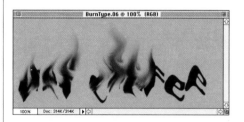

135

It's more fun to keep the top layer visible.

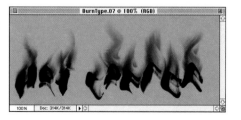

## VARIATIONS

Before you flatten or merge the layers, try some other blending modes. Here's Overlay at 100%.

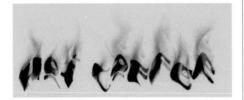

Saturation mode at 100%.

Difference mode at 65%. ■

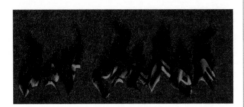

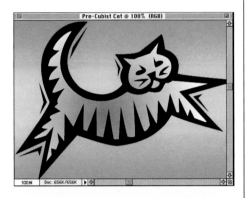

Sharron Evans created an experimental technique that I used to make an effect similar to the Cubist paintings of the early 20th Century. It's the single-pixel-column-and-row-arrow-drag method. We've got to come up with a snappier name than that.

This technique works best with high-contrast images. I'm using the EPS image "Cat," found in the Image Club➡Woodcuts folder on your *Photoshop Effects Magic* CD-ROM. I added color gradients and called the result "Pre-Cubist Cat." It's on the CD-ROM in the ArtStart folder.

**1** Double-click the Marquee tool and choose Single Column for the shape. Hold down the Shift key and click the image several times to establish an irregular array of vertical selection lines.

**2** Now hold down the (Option) [Alt] and (Command)[Control] keys while you click the keyboard's Right arrow 10 to 15 times. It may take a few seconds for your computer to complete this action.

**3** Change to the single row Marquee tool and Shift-click several horizontal selection lines.

**4** Repeat Step 2, this time clicking the Up or Down arrow to alter the image further. Your cat may look something like this.

## VARIATIONS

Wondering how to do the maneuver with diagonal lines? Rotate the canvas. Here's "Dog" from the Image Club→Woodcuts folder on your Effects Magic CD-ROM.

I used Image→Rotate Canvas→ Arbitrary and typed in 45°. I chose clockwise arbitrarily because I'll rotate it back in the opposite direction when I'm finished.

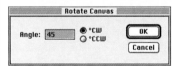

I repeated the single-pixel drag technique for rows and columns, exactly as I did for "Cat." Then I returned the image to horizontal with the Rotate Canvas command. Rotating results in a lot of white space around the image, so I cropped it.

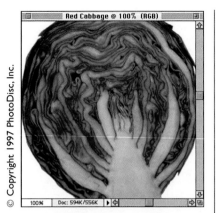

The larger the spaces between the rows or columns, and the greater the number of clicks on the arrow keys, the more abstract the image becomes.

I'm using a photograph this time. "Cabbage" is on the book's CD-ROM in the PhotoDisc folder. The image has intriguing organic shapes.

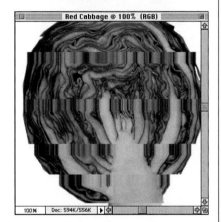

I used only four rows of selection lines and I moved them about 30 pixels.

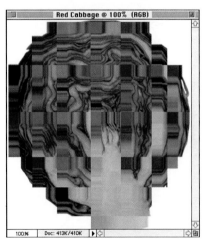

Then I used seven vertical colums and dragged them 30 pixels. The combination of geometric and organic shapes is intriguing.

To add some illusion of 3-D I used
Filter➡Stylize➡Extrude, with the
settings shown. ■

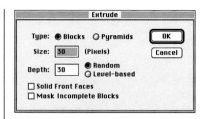

I wasn't sure what to name this section. "Grainy, Flaky, and Crumbly" sounded too much like a law firm.

These techniques work best with fonts that are already somewhat fragmented. Image Club's Fragile and Fajita are crumbly and flaky right out of the box, so we have a head start. I like the idea of pushing or exaggerating what's already there. If you want proof of that, see "Caricature" (page 34).

You need to install the fonts before launching Photoshop. Yes, they're both in the Image Club folder on the *Photoshop Effects Magic* CD-ROM, or just open the "fragile" file and skip to Step 4.

**1** Create a new file about 5×2 inches and fill it with a fairly dark color. I used a burgundy with CMYK values 51, 88, 12, 15.

**2** Switch the foreground and background colors to make white the foreground color. Select the Type tool icon and click anywhere on your image to access the Type Tool dialog box. Select a font and point size. Type your text and click OK.

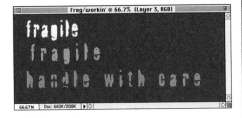

Repeat Step 2, using a light color such as this green (CMYK 45, 0, 45, 0). Increase the letter spacing. I used 8 points.

For the third line choose a foreground color of white and keep the same letter-spacing. Reduce the opacity of the layer to 50%.

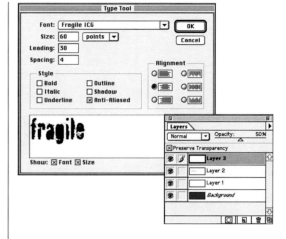

**3** Each line of type exists on its own layer. Use Layer➟Transform commands to resize, rotate, and reposition them. Flatten the image.

**TIP** Use Free Transform to make more than one change on a given layer, or use the keyboard shortcut (Command-T)[Control-T].

**4** Apply Filter➟Brush Strokes➟ Spatter (Radius 14, Smoothness 5). This will scatter pixels in the type, making the words practically illegible.

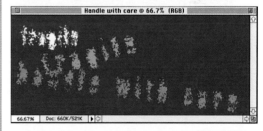

143

**5** Choose Filter➟Fade to fade the effect to about 50%. Save the image in preparation for the next step.

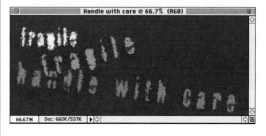

**6** Apply Filter➡Texture➡ Craquelure, using these settings. This creates a crumbly look with depth resulting from shadows and highlights.

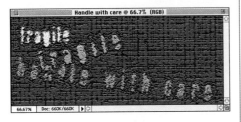

**7** The effect will be more dramatic if you eliminate or tone down most of the cracks in the "wall" around the type. Use the Eraser tool with Erase to Saved checked, and vary the pressure as you restore smoothness to parts of the wall.

## VARIATIONS

Combining Film Grain and Spatter filters can make type look like sand. Open "Beach" in the ArtStart folder on the CD-ROM, or create it yourself.

**1** Create a new file about 3×1.5 inches. Fill with a sunny yellow with CMYK values 9, 6, 99, 1.

**2** Choose for the foreground color a dark brown such as CMYK 31, 59, 88, 43. Enter the text in Fajita font.

**3** Apply Filter➡Artistic➡Film Grain (Grain 12, Highlight 20, Intensity 10) to the type layer. Now the letters look as if they are cut from sandpaper.

**4** Flatten the image. Apply Filter➡Brush Strokes➡Spatter (Radius 12, Smoothness 4). Select Filter➡Fade to fade the Spatter effect until the type is legible, using Dissolve mode to enhance the graininess.

Adding a blast of wind produces a sandstorm.

Apply Filter➡Stylize➡Wind (Blast), using either direction. Fade to taste, using Dissolve mode. ■

Here's how to add color to clip art and create the illusion of speedy movement using a combination of Photoshop techniques.

**1** Create a new file. Mine is 7×5 inches at 72 dpi.

**2** Open or Place the images you want to work with. I am using the EPS images "Fries" and "Burger." You'll find them in the Image Club folder on the *Photoshop Effects Magic* CD-ROM.

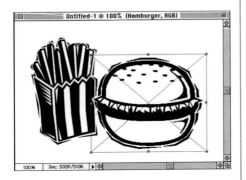

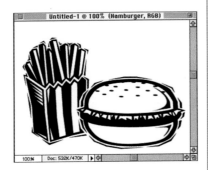

**3** Make the Hamburger layer active. Select Layer➥Free Transform. This puts a bounding box with handles around the burger. Move the top-center handle down to reduce the vertical size of the hamburger.

**4** Make the French Fries layer active. If it is not already behind the hamburger, use Layer➥Arrange to send it backward.

 **Layers can be rearranged by dragging them up or down in the Layers palette.**

146

**5** Transform the fries to make them a little more cartoon-like and active. Use Layer➡Transform➡ Perspective to get a higher camera angle and Layer➡Transform➡ Rotate to make the fries lean to the left. Flatten the image.

**6** Use the Fill Bucket to add flat color to the white areas in the graphics. Here are the CMYK values I used: French fries bag: 0, 91, 100, 0; French fries, dark areas: 26, 36, 92, 19; French fries, light areas: 11, 27, 91, 2; burger, beef and outline: 45, 36, 95, 53; lettuce: 73, 0, 96, 0.

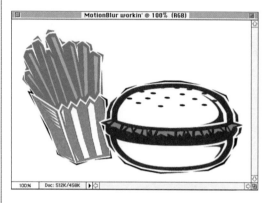

**7** Use the Eyedropper to pick up the golden color that was used for the French fries' dark areas. Select the white area of the top half of the bun with the Magic Wand tool. Double-click the Gradient tool to display the Gradient Tool Options floating palette. Use these settings.

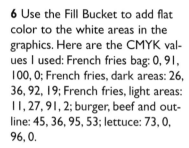

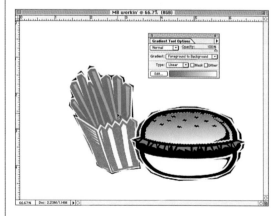

147

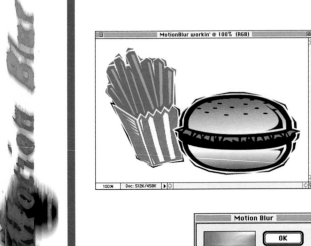

**8** Click the Gradient tool at the top center of the bun and drag straight down to the bottom of the selection. Repeat for the lower half of the bun, but drag upward from the bottom. Here's the image fully colored.

**9** Apply Filter➡Blur➡Motion Blur (Angle: 0, Distance: 70) to the entire image. Do not save.

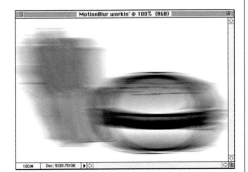

**10** Double-click the Eraser tool to open the Eraser Options palette and set it to Erase to Saved. Use the Eraser to remove portions of the blur. Using Airbrush mode at 25-50% pressure with a large brush enables you to bring back the saved edges on the right side of the French fries and the hamburger softly. Use tiny brush sizes to create streaks of the original across the blur. When you're happy with the effect, save the image.

I need more white space on the left before the next maneuver, so I can add some with the Image➡Canvas Size command.

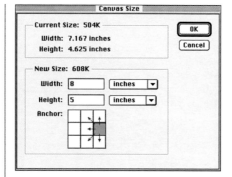

**11** Select the fries by throwing a loose lasso around them. Include plenty of white space, as shown. Then choose Select➡Feather (12 pixels).

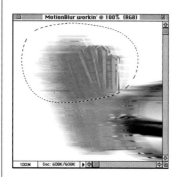

**12** Choose Filter➡Distort➡Shear and adjust the curve to make the fries appear to be "blowing" toward the left.

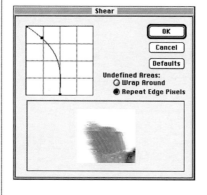

149

All done. Have some lunch. Maybe the next version of Photoshop will have a cholesterol filter! ■

The Pen tool and the Paths palette are used here to create a tulip garden.

**1** Open "Tulip" in the ArtStart folder on the *Photoshop Effects Magic* CD-ROM.

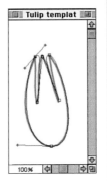

**2** Use the Pen tool to make a path for the outline of the tulip. Start by clicking on the tip of the left-hand petal and dragging slightly down and to the left. Next click the bottom curve and then drag to the right. Continue around the shape, clicking without dragging, and finish by clicking again on the first point. Don't worry if your path doesn't match the template yet.

**3** Drag to select the Direct Selection tool in the toolbox. Adjust the curves and points of your path as you want. Use the Save Path command in the Paths palette menu to save the working path as "Tulip."

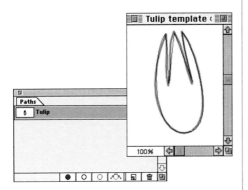

**4** Create a new file for your tulip garden. Mine is 4×2 inches. Drag and drop Tulip from the Paths palette of the template to the new image window.

**5** Choose bright colors for both the foreground and the background. Red with CMYK values 0, 90, 90, 0, and lavender with CMYK values 34, 60, 0, 0 will do nicely for our first tulip. Choose "fill path" from the Paths pop-up menu. Notice that you can choose to fill with any percentage of the foreground, background, black or white. Use 75% of the foreground color.

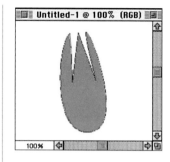

To see how the fill looks, turn off the path using the Paths palette menu (but don't delete it!)

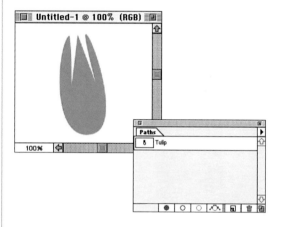

**6** Copy the path to several new locations by selecting it in the Paths palette and clicking on its outline in the image with the Direct Selection tool. Hold down the (Option)[Alt] key as you drag the path.

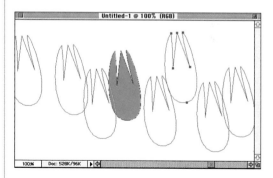

151

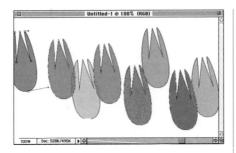

**7** Fill all the paths with a variety of shades of the foreground and background colors.

I'll stroke (outline) all the tulips at the same time. First I'll choose a brush tip.

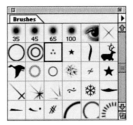

**8** Load Assorted Brushes and choose the brush shown here.

**9** Select all the paths by dragging a rectangle around them with the Direct Selection tool.

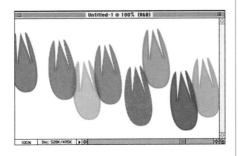

**10** Choose the Burn tool from the Stroke Path menu. This results in a slightly darker edge around each tulip.

All you neeed now are stems and leaves.

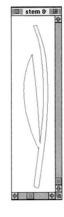

**11** Open "Stem & Leaf path" in the ArtStart folder on the CD-ROM.

**12** Drag and Drop the path name from the Paths palette to your tulips image, and make all the copies you need with the (Option-click)[Alt-click] and drag maneuver.

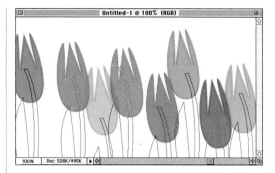

**13** Use the Direct Selection tool to reshape the curves and position the anchor points of each stem and leaf. Notice that you can work with path elements even if they are outside the image's "live" area.

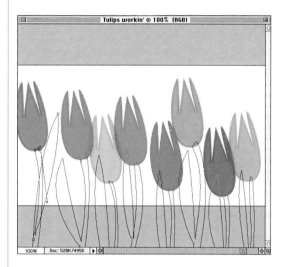

**14** I chose to add another ½-inch of canvas to the bottom of the image, using Image➥Canvas Size.

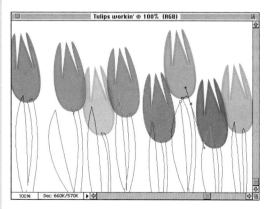

153

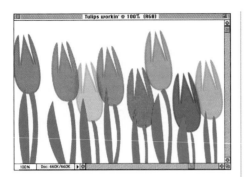

**15** Select the paths by dragging with the Direct Selection tool and fill all the stems and leaves using 100% green with CMYK values 78, 0, 98, 0.

## VARIATIONS

Numerous variations are possible with the same paths you have. Just change the fill and stroke variables.

This version has all the tulips filled with 100% pink CMYK values 9, 57, 0, 1. I made the stroke with red after offsetting the paths a few pixels and using the brush shown. I used the "three-dot" brush to stroke the stems and leaves with a darker green than the fill, but I did not offset the paths.

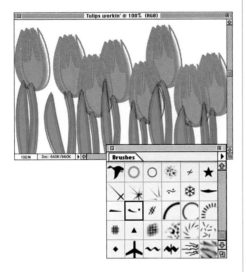

Here's the result of opening up one of the tulips by adding anchor points for the outer petals and converting their tips to smooth points. I copied the open flower several times and filled them with yellow.

I resized one of the new flowers by converting it into a selection so it could be scaled by the Layer➡ Transform command. I pasted this smaller flower into a new path on the same document, where I copied it several times and filled it with orange in Multiply mode. The stems were done quickly with the Line tool at 7 or 9 points wide. ▩

If you want to add color to a line art feast, Darken Mode is your friend because it enables you to be sloppy without messing up the line work. This technique is useful for roughs and comps or a spontaneous, casual look in finished art.

1 Create a new file 4×2 inches.

2 Open or place your line art image. I'm using the EPS clip art "Cappuccino" and "Croissant." You'll find them in the Image Club folder on the *Photoshop Effects Magic* CD-ROM.

3 Use Layer➡Free Transform to adjust each images size and position. Use the Escape key to cancel a transformation. Press (Return) [Enter] when you are satisfied. It may take a few maneuvers, including rotation and vertical size reduction, to make the croissant look as if it is lying on the table. Now the fun part—applying color!

**4** I chose CMYK 24, 40, 88, 13 for a toasty tan color. Double-click the Airbrush tool to open the Airbrush Options palette and set it for Darken mode, then spray some color on the croissant. Vary your pressure. Notice that the black lines are unaffected because they are already darker than the tone you are adding.

 **There's no need to be precise with your application of color. The style of the original line art is casual and quick. Use a similar attitude when tossing in some color.**

**5** Airbrush a bit of cinnamon and chocolate onto the foam, using the same color and technique.

**6** Switch to a different color for the cup and saucer. I used a blue composed of these CMYK values: 42, 0, 1, 0. Use a Fat brush and make sure you stay in Darken mode. Paint the cup with vertical strokes that fade out as you go from left to right (and vice versa) to leave a highlight on the cup. Vary pressure to achieve this "casual gradient" effect.

Mouse users may find using the Fade box and typing in a large number of steps the ideal way to achieve the "casual gradient." I used 60 steps. With this method tablet users won't need to change stylus pressure during the stroke.

**7** The mocha-flavored steam rising from the foam is made with the Smudge tool. I used about 50% pressure in Normal mode and made a few zigzag drags going up and fading out.

## VARIATIONS

I added some casual color to the "Spanish Coffee" clip art in the "Sketches on the Town" folder on the CD-ROM.

Untitled-1 @ 100% (Spa

This time I wanted to color the black areas and leave the white untouched. It's no problem using Lighten mode.

Here's the clip art "Lobster" from Image Club. I applied quick strokes of red with a fat Paintbrush in Darken mode. I also checked the Wet Edges checkbox to get the look of watercolor, with pigment pooling up around the brush strokes.

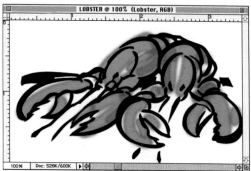

I added some strokes and dabs in light orange and lavender, using Multiply mode. Multiply mode does not disturb the black outlines but does allow light colors to influence darker ones. ▪

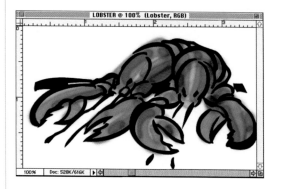

159

To preserve transparency or not to preserve transparency—that is the question. The answer depends on what you want to do to the image.

With Preserve Transparency turned on, transparent pixels cannot be changed in any way. If you want to change the color of type on a layer, for example, turn Preserve Transparency on to restrict color to the type. If you want to alter the shape of the type, you should turn Preserve Transparency off so that the pixels can change without restriction.

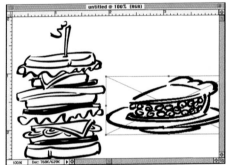

**1** EPS clip art is ideal because the "white" areas are actually transparent. I placed "Big Sandwich" and "Pie" (from the Image Club➡ Sketches folder of your *Photoshop Effects Magic* CD-ROM). Each placed image resides on its own layer, automatically named.

**2** To change the black line art to a color, turn on Preserve Transparency for its layer and fill the layer with the new foreground color. I used green with CMYK values 81, 28, 100, 22 for the Sandwich layer and blue with CMYK values 91, 68, 8, 3 on the Pie layer. Only the lines will be affected because everything else is transparent.

**TIP** Press (Option-delete)[Alt-delete] to fill the selection with foreground color.

Want proof that the white areas of the images are transparent? Make the Background layer invisible and the telltale checkerboard appears.

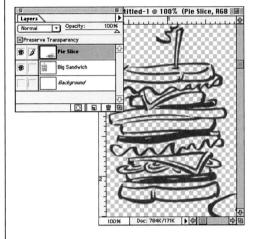

**3** To color transparent areas, you will have to turn off Preserve Transparency. Use the Paint Bucket to fill sections that are completely enclosed. Switch to the Brush tool to paint in areas that have "leaks," such as the pie crust or the lettuce in the middle of the sandwich.

**TIP** If you are painting with colors that are lighter than the green or blue outlines, use **Darken** mode. This makes it easier to avoid covering the outlines accidentally. Painting in Darken mode is also a great way to touch up edges that weren't completely filled with the Paint Bucket.

**4** Enter some text. To change the color of the type without affecting the transparent pixels that make up the rest of the layer, turn on Preserve Transparency. Then use any technique you like for filling or painting the letters.

When you distort type, turn off Preserve Transparency.

**5** Make a rectangular selection around the type. This will establish the center for the effect and prevent the computer from trying to distort all those transparent pixels! Apply Filter➡Distort➡Spherize (75%, Normal).

**6** Just for fun, repeat Step 5 but turn on Preserve Transparency. The distortion cannot be seen in the transparent areas surrounding the original type.

# VARIATIONS

With Preserve Transparency, you can do much more than simply switch colors. You can paint or draw with no fear of going outside the lines. Here's some "plain" type.

This satin finish was created by the Airbrush in some pastel colors dragged across the whole word.

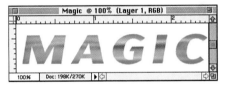

There may be times when you'll deliberately ignore the rule to turn off Preserve Transparency before using a distortion filter. I applied a displacement map to the type with Preserve Transparency on.

Then I used the Fade command to switch to multiply mode. ■

163

# PART III

## Starting from Scratch

You don't need to begin with a photo, clip art, or type. You can create amazing effects in Photoshop starting with a blank canvas. Here's where you'll learn how to exploit Photoshop's power as a painting program.

You'll use and create custom brushes and paint with light, gradients, and textures. You'll make patterns and abstract art. You'll even learn to make digital frames for your artwork. Finally, you'll discover a great way to recycle traditional art materials.

Four of these techniques work much better if you have a graphics tablet: "Bristle Brush," "Rough Sketch," "Textured Brush," and "Cobblestones." I hate to nag, but you should really get a tablet already.

Just about anything can serve as raw material for Photoshop art. A scribble. A doodle. Scan some art by a two-year-old (make sure she signs a release form).

Drawing circles is a good way to practice control of your stylus or your mouse. And when you fill an area with circles you have the first stage for colorful abstract art.

**I** Create a new file and choose a background color of white. Paint some circles in a variety of sizes and with an assortment of brushes. Or open "Circles" in the ArtStart folder on the *Photoshop Effects Magic* CD-ROM.

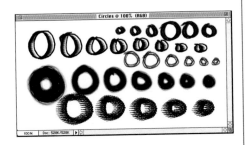

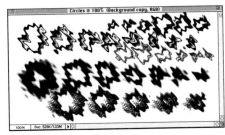

**2** Duplicate the layer and apply a filter effect to this Background Copy. I used Filter➡Distort➡Ripple (200, Large).

**TIP** When you expect to be exploring a number of variations of a single source image it's convenient to "stack" them as layers. You can quickly see how any combination of layers looks by controlling the visibility, opacity, and blending modes. Use the **Save As** command for the versions you want to keep.

**3** Rename the Background Copy layer "Ripple 200," or whatever describes the effect you used.

166

**4** Duplicate the original layer again. I'm naming the new layer "Pinch 100" because that's the next effect I plan to use. Here's the Pinch layer at 100% opacity, covering up the original (Background) circle layer. The Ripple layer is invisible for the moment.

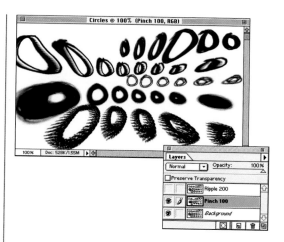

Let's throw in some color.

**5** Make the Ripple layer visible and active. Use the Transparent Rainbow Gradient preset. I used these settings. Darken mode produces rich color without affecting the black areas.

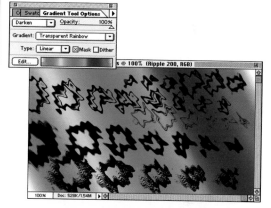

**6** Make the Ripple layer invisible and the Pinch layer active. Change the gradient type to Radial. I dragged from the middle of the image to the edge.

167

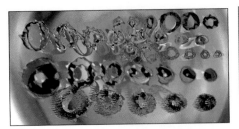

Now you're ready to play around with combinations. I ended up with this for my final image.

The Layers palette shows Exclusion is the Blending mode for the Ripples layer. I used Difference mode for the Pinch layer.

# VARIATIONS

We'll start with a scribble and turn it into embossed string-art.

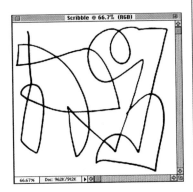

Make a scribble with the Brush tool or use my "Scribble" in the ArtStart folder on the CD-ROM. I used a single stroke with no variation in pressure. Lots of curves and angles crossing each other at several points create a variety of interesting shapes.

Use the Paint Bucket tool to fill all the shapes and the background with various colors. I used a Tolerance of 100 in the Paint Bucket Options.

See "Cartoons" (page 122) for tips on filling line art with flat color.

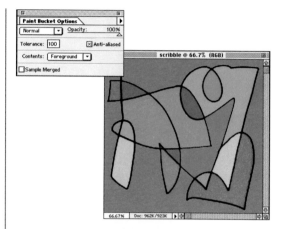

Apply Filter➡Stylize➡Emboss (Angle: 143, Height: 6, Amount: 104). All your fills become gray, but the line stands out in multicolor relief.

Here's an alternative to the Emboss effect. I applied Filter➡Distort➡ Polar Coordinates (Rectangular to Polar) to the colored scribble.

169

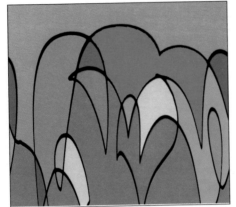

The results are quite different with the Polar to Rectangular conversion.

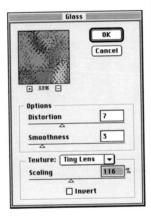

Or, apply Filter➡Distort➡Glass with these settings:

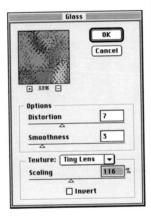

Crop out the excess background to focus on the great optical effects that would make any shower curtain proud!

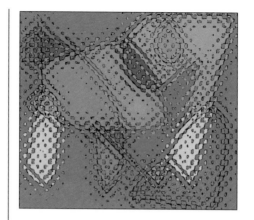

If you like Polar Coordinates effects, see "Unconventional Tools" (page 210). ■

You may already be using some of the alternative brush sets included with Photoshop. If not, this is as good a time as any to try some. And you'll learn how to make custom brushes from scratch. This is especially useful if you don't have Fractal Design Painter, or don't want to switch back and forth between Painter and Photoshop so often. This technique works best with a tablet and stylus.

The default brushes comprise 16 round tips, hard- or soft-edged, in various sizes.

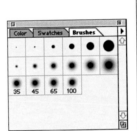

**1** Load Assorted Brushes.

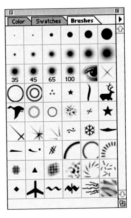

**2** Experiment with some of these brushes. You might not always be able to predict what their strokes will look like just by looking at their "footprints."

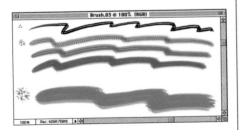

The "3-dots" brush makes a sketchy line. You can explore it further in the "Rough Sketch" technique. See page 198.

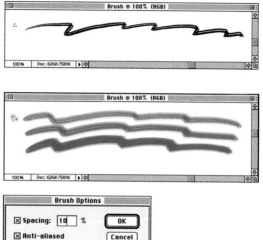

**3** The first stroke in this group was made by the brush I call Medium Bristles, and it looks like tire tracks. We can change that.

Find Brush Options in the Brushes palette menu. (This is not the same as the Paintbrush Options palette.) Change the default spacing to a lower value. I used 10% for the next stroke, making a dry brush look. Lower the spacing to the minimum 1% to get a smoother stroke, as if the brush is loaded with paint.

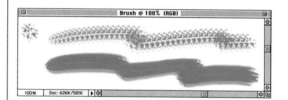

These 2 strokes were made with the "Large Bristle" brush, which is identical to the previous one except for its size. It makes "tire tracks," too, but from a truck. Again, change the spacing to a low enough percentage to get a smooth effect. I used 3% here.

Let's create a new brush.

**1** Open a new grayscale file about 4×4 inches at 72 dpi.

**2** Double-click the Line tool and enter 1 point for line width. Accept the other default variables.

**3** Hold down the Shift key for perfect horizontals and make several short strokes as close together as you can. Make sure you leave a little white space between the strokes. Each of these 1-pixel lines will become a "bristle" in your brush.

173

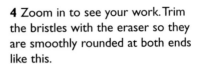

**4** Zoom in to see your work. Trim the bristles with the eraser so they are smoothly rounded at both ends like this.

**5** Drag a selection rectangle around the lines. Choose Define Brush from the arrow menu of the Brushes palette. Voilà! Your new brush occupies a space in the palette.

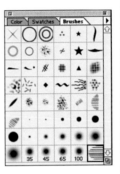

The Brushes palette shown here contains the basic default set plus "Magic Brushes" in the ArtStart folder on the *Photoshop Effects Magic* CD-ROM.

**6** Remember to change the annoying default 25% spacing to a lower number in the Brush Options box.

Test your new brush with a zigzag drag. It looks streaky like a "dry" brush when you drag horizontally, but full of paint when you drag in any other direction.

## VARIATIONS

You can probably guess how to make a brush tip that looks streaky when you drag vertically. Go back to step 5. Before you use the Define Brush command, go to Layer➡Transform➡Rotate 90° CW.

I made eight vertical drags with this new version. Then I switched to the Eraser tool, keeping the same brush, and dragged over the first four strokes.

To make the background design for this section's thumbtab I filled an area with the Yellow, Violet, Orange, Blue gradient and used the Smudge tool (75% pressure) with my new vertical bristle tip. I alternated downward and upward drags through the colors.

Once you have a horizontal bristle brush it's easy to make motion blur effects just by dragging the Smudge tool across the image. Each stroke should go in the same direction. ■

Didn't you love to pop the bubbles when they came wrapped around something fragile? Don't you still love to? A single circular selection becomes the basic element for a 3-D pattern, and its "op-art" variations.

**1** Create a new file 2×2 inches, 72 dpi. Use View➤Show Grid and View➤Snap To Grid. I'm using a gridline every inch, and a subdivision every ¼ inch. Use File➤Preferences➤Guides & Grid if you need to adjust your grid.

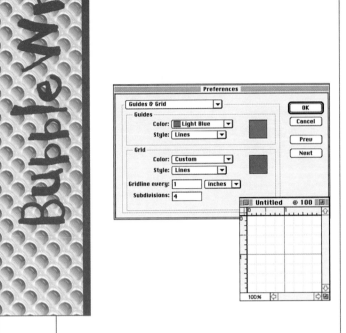

Normally I hate precision, but exactitude will be helpful in creating the pattern tile.

**2** Use the elliptical Marquee. Place your cursor at the center of one of the grid quadrants and hold down the (Option)[Alt] and Shift keys. Drag to make a perfect circle $\frac{1}{4}$ inch in diameter.

**3** Double-click the Gradient tool to open the Gradient Tool Options palette and choose these settings.

**4** Switch to default colors. Drag the gradient line from the lower-right edge of the circle through the center and finish at the upper-left edge. Your "bubble" is lit from the top-left.

**5** Use Layer➡Transform➡Numeric to increase the size of the circle by 125%.

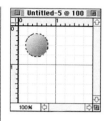

This is the basic element of the pattern. Next you'll prepare the tile for a seamless fill.

**6** Copy the shaded circle into each of the other quadrants by holding down the (Command)[Control] and (Option)[Alt] keys while dragging the circle into place. Drag another copy to the exact center of the image window. The Snap To Grid function will help your accuracy.

**7** Use the rectangular Marquee to make a selection like this.

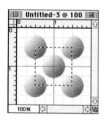

**8** Select Edit➡Define Pattern to establish your selection as a pattern fill.

**9** Create a new file and use Edit➡Fill, choosing Pattern for the contents.

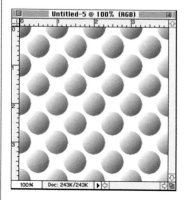

177

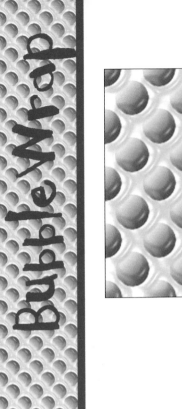

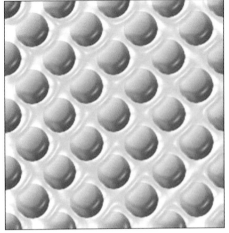

**10** Finally, apply Filter➡Artistic➡ Plastic Wrap (Highlight 11, Detail 6, Smoothness 10).

## VARIATIONS

I used these settings in the Gradient Tool Options palette to add a metallic look.

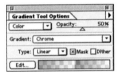

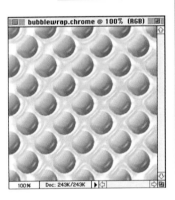

After Step 9, fill with a gradient in Color mode. Then apply Filter➡ Distort➡Spherize (100%) and get this op-art design.

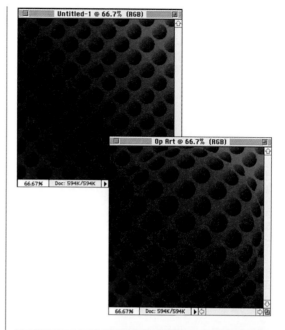

If you omit the center bubble in Step 6, your pattern fill consists of columns and rows. I've also added a solid color fill in Multiply mode.

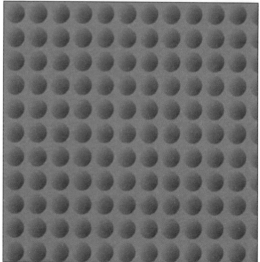

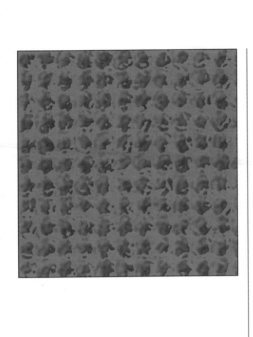

Then I applied Filter➡Distort➡ Ocean Ripple (Size 6, Magnitude 7) to produce this pattern of blobs.

To have more space around each bubble, skip Step 5.

Take this "more space" variation, and fill the columns with color, using a different apply mode for each. I used CMYK values of 58, 0, 15, 0 for the foreground color.

**1** Select the leftmost column with a rectangular marquee. Select Edit➡Fill using Color mode at 50%.

**2** Select the next column and fill using Darken mode at 35%.

 **TIP** No need to redraw the marquee for each column, just drag the marching ants to the right.

**3** For the third column, use Lighten mode at 100%.

**4** In the fourth column, apply the Difference mode at 25%.

**5** Finally, fill the last column with Color Burn mode at 75%. ■

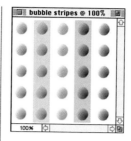

Texture is often added to enhance an image. Here's how to make a "patchwork" where visual interest is created from variety in direction, size, and intensity of the texture alone.

**1** Create a new file. Mine is a strip approximately 1×3 inches at 150 dpi.

**2** Double-click the Selection Marquee tool and use these settings in the Marquee Options palette. Each time you click in the document, a perfect 100 pixel square is selected.

**3** Make your first click.

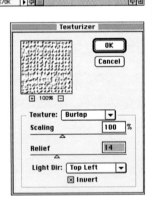

**4** Choose Filter➡Texture➡ Texturizer. Use these settings to create your first square.

I made a strip of burlap "swatches," which varied in the scale, direction, and depth of the weave. Make up your own combinations as you go or use my settings.

Burlap remains the choice for the entire sequence. Percentage given refers to size of the texture and numbers from zero to 50 indicate the amount or darkness of the effect. Finally, choice of lighting direction is indicated.

 **TIP** **(Command-Option-F) [Control-Alt-F] opens the Texturizer dialog box again.**

These settings will fill out the first strip:

Square 2: 69%, 9, Top Left

Square 3: 100%, 12, Left

Square 4: 50%, 7, Bottom Right

For the second strip use these settings:

Square 1: 108%, 12, Top Left

Square 2: 80%, 21, Left

Square 3: 175%, 13, Bottom

Square 4: 140%, 23, Right

The third strip was created as follows:

Square 1: 93%, 32, Bottom

Square 2: 50%, 16, Top Left

Square 3: 150%, 21, Bottom Right, Invert

Square 4: 69%, 11, Bottom Right

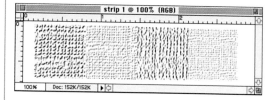

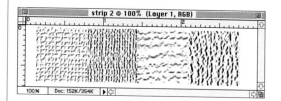

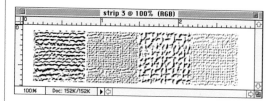

183

Here's the fourth strip:

Square 1: 140%, 10, Bottom

Square 2: 200%, 10, Top Left

Square 3: 117%, 10, Top

Square 4: 117%, 29, Top Right

To stitch your patchwork quilt together:

**1** Open strip1. Select Image➡ Canvas Size. Increase the vertical dimension to about 3 inches, with the current image at the top as shown. This creates space below the strip.

**2** Drag and drop each of the other strips into place.

## VARIATIONS

You can add color in several ways to your patchwork:

**1** Continue using the 100-pixel square selection marquee. Just click it over the texture swatch you want to color.

**2** I used these CMYK values and selected Edit➥Fill with these blending modes:

red: 0, 81, 68, 0; Color mode (100%);

purple: 62, 66, 0, 0; Hard Light (50%)

gold: 9, 28, 98, 0; Darken (100%)

blue-green: 56, 0, 25, 0; Darken (50%)

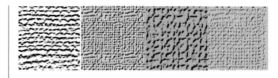

Here is the same strip and the same colors, but this time I used the Paintbrush with the wet edges box checked to get a watercolor look. The blending mode is Normal at 50%.

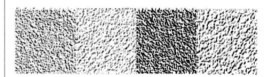

Use the sandstone texture instead of burlap. ■

This technique is useful for anyone who doesn't have time to search for the perfect stone background in their CD-ROM library of Stock images. It's a quick way to create a fill pattern for layouts or comps— or final art if you're going for a hand-drawn look.

**1** To begin the pattern tile I created a new file in grayscale 1-inch square at 72 dpi and filled it with medium gray.

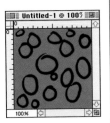

**2** Choose a foreground color of black. With the Brush tool, draw irregular circles of various sizes, randomly arranged.

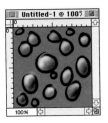

**3** Switch the foreground color to white. With the Airbrush tool at 25–35% pressure, add highlights and shadows to indicate a light source from the upper-left corner.

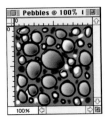

**4** When you're satisfied with the stones it's ready to become a tile for a pattern fill.

**5** Depending on the size and resolution of the image you want to fill, you may want to change the size of the tile. I reduced mine to about 50% size with Layer➡Transform➡ Scale.

**6** The small tile is still selected. Use Edit➡Define Pattern to make this the element of a pattern fill.

**7** Create a new file or open an image that could use a cobblestone path or wall. I wanted to create a "worm's eye view" for this cartoon of a Medieval knight on a high stone wall. You'll find "Wallguy" in the ArtStart folder on the *Photoshop Effects Magic* CD-ROM.

**8** Create a new layer (Layer 1) for the pattern. Make a selection in Layer 1 and fill it with the pattern. I dragged a rectangular Marquee approximately the height and width of the stone wall in my layout.

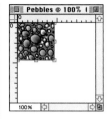

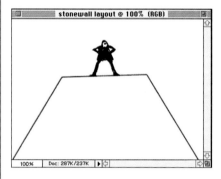

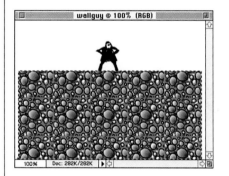

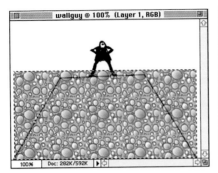

**9** I reduced the opacity of Layer 1 so I could see the outline of the wall. I used Layer➡Transform➡Distort to create the illusion of perspective.

**TIP** **There is a Perspective option in the Transform commands but it does not enable you to manipulate the handles on the image independently. The Distort option does just that, giving you more control in one step. ∎**

Create a variety of electronic frames for your Photoshop art. The Border command is your digital mitre box!

**1** Create a new file 3×2 inches. Choose a foreground color and fill the file with a dark color. I used reddish brown with CMYK values 0, 100, 0, 40.

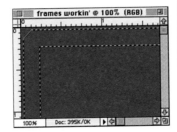

**2** Make the rulers visible with (Command-R)[Control-R]. Drag a rectangular selection marquee about ⅛ inch from the edges of the window. Select➥Modify➥ Border (35 pixels). This creates a frame-like selection border with mitred corners and a preset gradient that will show up when you fill the selection with a color.

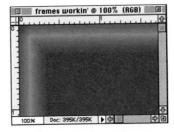

**3** Choose a foreground color for your fill. Mine is light tan (CMYK 0, 25, 50, 25). Select Edit➥Fill at 100% normal.

**4** Switch to default colors. Select the interior of the frame and insert some artwork with the Paste Into command, like this tropical sunset from PhotoDisc. I also cropped the frame just enough to enhance the mitred corner effect.

## VARIATIONS

This "bleached oak" look resulted from increasing the brightness (+35) and decreasing contrast (−44) after Step 3. I also trimmed off more of the outer frame and I added a bevel-cut mat.

Here's how to make a textured mat in a wide strip inside the frame.

**1** Select the area and apply Filter➥ Texture➥Texturizer. I used Canvas.

**2** Choose a foreground color of light cream or pink and use Edit➥Fill in Color mode, so the white remains but the nubby texture has more realism. I used 50% opacity.

**3** Drag a rectangular Marquee around the inside edge of the mat and use Edit➥Stroke to create the beveled edge of the mat.

Multiple borders and strokes can create some complex traditional frames. After Step 3 I added a narrower border just inside the first one.

191

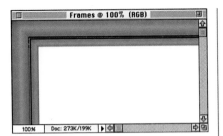

Drag a selection rectangle at the juncture between borders. Edit➡ Stroke using Center location with any foreground color and line weight.

**TIP** **Those double-strokes come out perfectly when you use an odd number of pixels (such as 5 or 7) and a single pixel in a contrasting color for the second stroke. Multiple fills will be perfectly centered if you use the Select➡Modify➡ Expand (or ➡Contract) commands.**

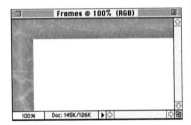

There are plenty of ways to add a wood-grain or other texture to your frame. This marbleized look comes from cutting a slab of "rawmeat" from the PhotoDisc file by that name. It's on the *Photoshop Effects Magic* CD-ROM. Just drag and drop it onto the "bleached oak" frame. I reduced the opacity of the Meat layer to about 20% and used Luminosity mode to eliminate the red color.

For the museum quality ornate gold I started with the Floral Medallion in the Image Club➡Objects folder on the CD-ROM.

192

I used the Single Column option of the selection Marquee to "extrude" the top of the frame by clicking on the right arrow of the keyboard while holding down the (Option-Command)[Alt-Control] keys. Yes, it takes lots and lots of clicks.

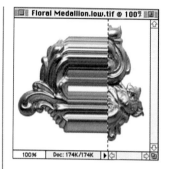

The corners consist of the original gold medallion, or parts of it blended together.

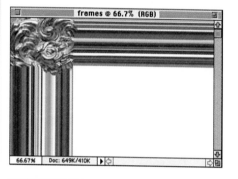

**TIP** Begin a file of virtual moldings. Crop out all but a 1- or 2-inch corner of the frame. It can be used to piece together a whole frame of any size. Better still, use File Info to enter descriptions or formulas for recreating each design. ■

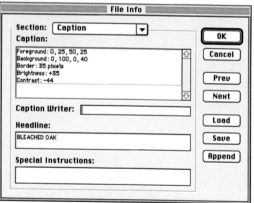

193

You don't need any fancy plug-ins to get these spectacular kaleido-scopic effects. They were all done with the Gradient tool. Begin with a radial fill and use Difference mode for additional fills. Incredible variety results from your choice of colors, the direction and length of the drag and the number of multiple fills. Opacity is another variable.

I used a 2-inch square for each of the designs. The recipes give you colors and dragging movements.

**1** Use the Blue, Red, Yellow gradient at 35% opacity, dragging from the center to any corner.

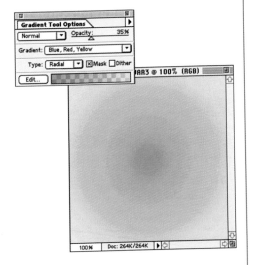

**2** Switch to default colors and use the Transparent Stripes gradient. Choose Difference mode in the Gradient Options palette. I kept opacity at 35%. Make a diagonal drag from one corner to the opposite corner of the image. Here's how my image looks after dragging from the lower-left to the upper-right corner.

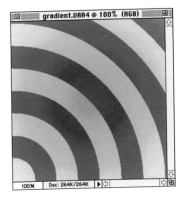

**3** Repeat for each of the other three corners of the image.

Here is the final image after all four diagonal fills have been applied.

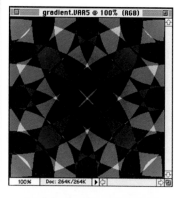

## Pastel Kaleidoscope

A delicate pastel-tinted design is the surprising result after a series of steps that cause increasingly darker images.

**1** Use the Yellow, Violet, Orange, Blue gradient in Normal mode at 100% opacity. Drag diagonally from the upper-left corner to the opposite corner.

**2** Use the Transparent Stripes gradient at 50% opacity. Remember to change to Difference mode. Drag from the center to any corner.

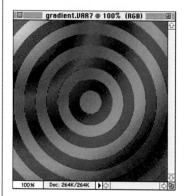

195

196

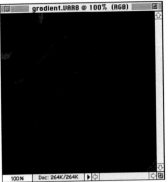

**3** Using the same settings, drag from one of the corners to the center. Repeat for the other three corners. Each successive drag makes the image darker.

To get the look of delicate water-color washes, use Image➡Adjust➡Invert to invert the colors (Command-I)[Control-I].

## VARIATIONS

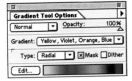

Make a seamless pattern tile with an abbreviated version of the kaleidoscope technique. Start with a radial fill in a 1×1-inch white square document. I'm using the Yellow, Violet, Orange, Blue gradient and dragging from the center to a corner.

When I used the radial fill with transparent stripes I used Difference mode again, but I switched the foreground color to white. I have no reason for that other than to add a little more variety. I made a diagonal drag from the lower-left to the upper-right corner.

My second drag went from the
upper-right to the lower-left corner.
This is the completed tile. Select➡
All and use Edit➡Define Pattern.

Use Edit➡Fill with Pattern at 100%
Normal in a larger document.  ■

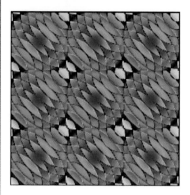

You can imitate the look of conventional art materials, such as bristle brushes (see page 172) and the scribbly pencil I'll use for this technique. Several Brush variables can be manipulated. The most important of these is the Brush tip.

**I** Load the Assorted Brushes. These new brush tips will appear below the default group as you scroll through the brushes.

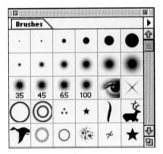

**2** Choose the brush tip that is made up of three dots arranged in a triangle.

Doodle with this new brush to get a feel for its sketchy quality. The three distinct points on the brush make lines that look as if they have been drawn over a couple of times, perhaps by an artist who was in too much of a hurry to erase. I recommend you use a rapid, loose style to take advantage of this rough quality in the tool. I made this series of squiggles using different settings in the Paintbrush Options palette.

The top squiggle was made with all of the boxes unchecked. I used my pressure-sensitive tablet for the rest. The next one used a fade of 150 steps. The third had Size as a function of pressure and the fourth had the Opacity box checked. In the next stroke, both Size and Opacity were a function of pressure.

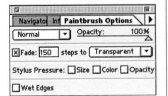

For the last two squiggles, I switched the background color to a bright red and had the Color box checked. This results in firm pressure producing the foreground (black) while lighter pressure fades to the background color.

**3** Roughly sketch a still life with this 3-dot brush. I used green with CMYK values 74, 0, 98, 0 to do this quick sketch of fruit. Normal mode at 100% opacity and only the Size box checked enables variation in stylus pressure to control the thickness of the stroke. My sketch is available in the ArtStart folder on the *Photoshop Effects Magic* CD-ROM.

**4** Add color and form using nothing but the 3-dot brush.

I roughed in color with quick strokes that followed the contours of the forms, more or less. The overlapping lines create additional shapes that can have different color fills for more visual interest. I purposely avoided solid fills, enabling the spaces between "bristles" to give the work spontaneity. Rather than undoing strokes, I sketched over them with different colors, which resulted in some nicely layered areas.

## VARIATIONS

Use the three-dot sketchy brush to work in Quick Mask mode. Draw from scratch or find an image to use as a template for tracing. I'm working with the "Fruit" image in the PhotoDisc folder on the CD-ROM.

**1** Enter Quick Mask mode. Roughly trace the outlines of the image.

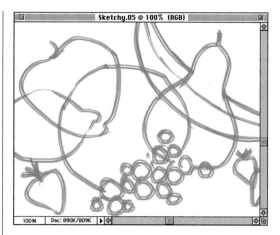

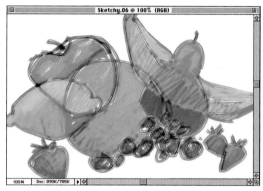

199

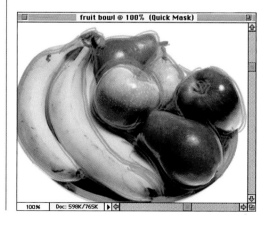

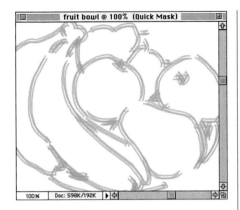

**2** Return to the composite channel. Select➡All and delete the image. Only the mask remains.

**3** Exit Quick Mask mode and the mask become a selection.

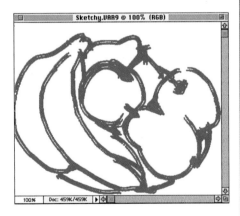

**4** The mask protects the outlines by default, so use Select➡Inverse to protect everything but the outlines. Use Edit➡Fill with a dark color. My choice is purple with CMYK values of 57, 58, 0, 0.

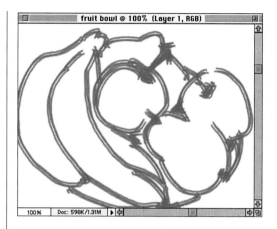

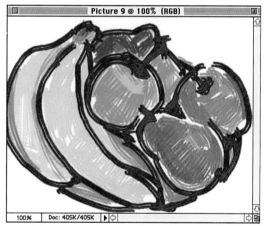

**5** Use Select➡Inverse again and the lines will be protected. Now you can get sloppy and energetic in your application of color and the lines won't be disturbed. ■

The Lighting Effects Filter provides controls for enhancing an image with a limitless combination of color, exposure, direction and placement of light sources, but you don't need to start with an image. Lights themselves can be all you need to create an image.

**1** Create a new file in RGB mode about 4 inches×3 inches and fill it with a linear gradient, dragging from the upper-left corner to the lower-right. I used CMYK values 5, 90, 0, 1 for the foreground color and CMYK values 61, 0, 22, 0 for the background color.

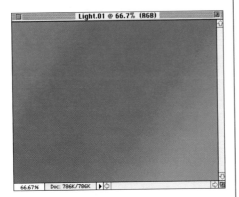

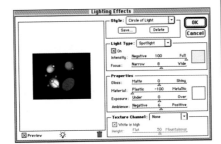

**2** Apply Filter➡Render➡Lighting Effects. Choose the "Circle of Light" style, accepting all default settings.

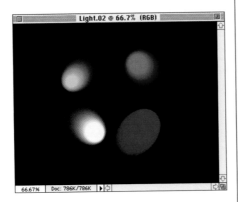

202

3 Choose Filter➡Fade and fade the effect to 60% with the Luminosity blending mode.

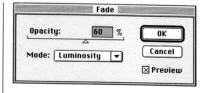

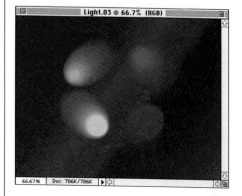

4 Select Filter➡Render➡Lighting Effects again to open the Lighting Effects dialog box. Because it was the last filter you had open, you can use the keyboard shortcut (Option-Command-F)[Alt-Control-F].

5 Choose the "Five Lights Down" style. You can move a light by clicking its source and then dragging it (the white spot in the preview image). Arrange three or four of the lights a bit more randomly.

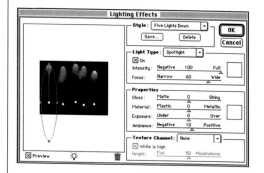

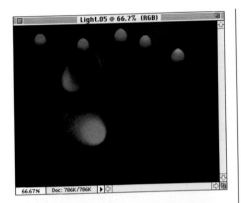

**6** Choose Filter➧Fade and switch the blending mode to Difference at 100% opacity.

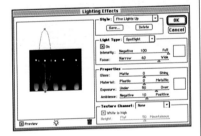

The five lights look like hooded figures, don't they? Repeat Step 5, arranging the lights below the first row. Use the Fade command at 100% opacity to apply the Screen mode. This keeps the image from becoming too dark.

**7** Repeat Step 4 and choose the "Five Lights Up" style. Move the white dots in the preview down slightly to arrange the lights at the lower edge of the image, like this:

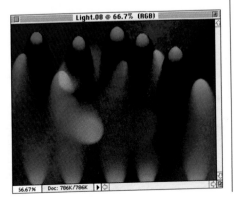

**8** Again, use the Fade command to find a blending mode that will reveal the previous stage. I used Exclusion at 75%.

**9** My final lighting effect is the "Soft Omni" style in Lighten mode. I also cropped away some of the lower part, to keep attention focused on the "figures."

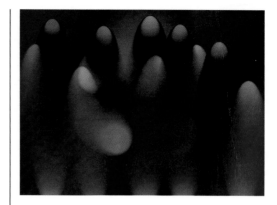

# VARIATIONS

The hardest part about experimental light-painting is knowing when you're done.

Here's a similar image, where I have added the "Triple Spotlight" to all the previous effects, using Screen mode in the Fade dialog box.

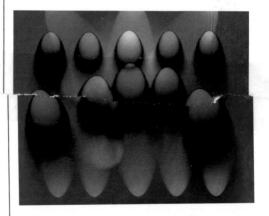

Filter➡Render➡Lens Flare (Brightness: 100, Lens Type: 50-300mm Zoom) makes the previous image look like this. I'll call that the finishing touch. ■

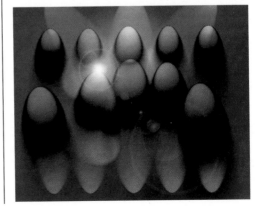

Sharron Evans created this technique for painting with color and texture in the same stroke. The method relies on Sharron's clever use of channels.

First, create a hand-made texture. Here's how I made one:

**1** Create a new file, a 1-inch square at 72 dpi.

**2** Fill the square with black.

**3** Switch the foreground color to white and make several vertical and horizontal strokes with the Brush tool in Dissolve mode. I used the brush size in the first column of the second row on the Brush palette.

**4** Choose Image➡Image Size (Height: .5 inches, Width: .5 inches). Reducing the texture swatch to a ¹/₂-inch square makes a finer weave.

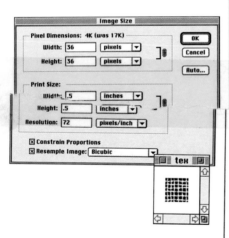

**5** Choose Select➡All then Edit➡Define Pattern to establish your texture as the fill pattern. It will remain available until you use Define Pattern on another selection.

**6** Create a new file 2×4 inches.

**7** Create a new channel (#4). Select Edit➠Fill using the pattern as content. You now have a texture mask.

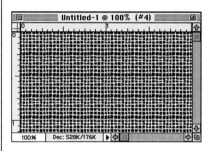

I could see the "tiling" of the repeating pattern, but it wasn't too bad. If you get serious tiling or breaks in the pattern, repeat Steps 2 through 7 until you're satisfied. Here's a good example, or rather a bad example, of a pattern element that needs to be redone.

**8** Load the selection Channel #4. Click OK and your pattern is filled with marching ants. Press (Command-H)[Control-H] to hide the marching ants without deselecting anything.

**9** Return to the composite channel. Choose a foreground color and a painting tool and make your mark. I used the calligraphy brush tip shown here, with the Brush tool in Dissolve mode to enhance the grainy quality.

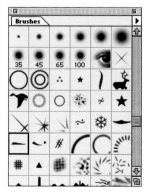

207

TIP Remember that this works only as long as the pattern in Channel #4 remains the active selection. If you want to make corrections in your work, use the Eraser rather than a select-and-delete maneuver.

## VARIATIONS

You don't need to make a texture from scratch. You can use the textures available in Photoshop 4.0's Texturizer menu.

**1** Create a new file 4×3 inches. Create a new channel for the texture mask.

**2** Selecting Filter➡Texture➡ Texturizer opens a dialog box for texture fills. Choose Brick for this example. Use my values for scale, relief, and light direction or try your own settings. The new channel is filled with a black-and-white brick pattern.

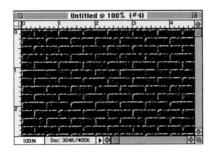

**3** Repeat Step 5, mentioned earlier. This time check the Invert box in the Load Selection dialog box before you click OK.

**4** Return to the composite channel. The image window is now white. Fill the selection with foreground color. I used CMYK values 32, 76, 60, 29 for a brick-red.

**5** Go ahead, scrawl some graffiti, too. I chose black as the foreground color and used a medium-sized Pencil. ■

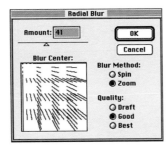

I still use conventional art materials, but I have to dust them off. If you've made a transition from traditional to digital art, you may wonder what to do with all your pens, pencils, markers, crayons, brushes, pastels, paint tubes, erasers, and so forth. You can still use them in your art, but they become the art rather than the method for creating it. I have scanned in my traditional tools to create an image that I can skew, filter, and modify. You can do the same, or use the image "Tools" in the ArtStart folder on the *Photoshop Effects Magic* CD-ROM.

**I** Apply Filter➤Blur➤Radial Blur. Use these settings and move the center of the blur to the upper-left corner.

**2** Choose Filter➟Fade, leaving the effect at 100% and switching to Difference mode. The blur creates a mysterious back-lighting.

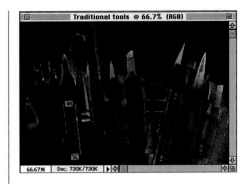

## VARIATIONS

Here's a completely different series of effects using the Polar Coordinates filter.

**1** Apply Filter➟Distort➟Polar Coordinates (Rectangular to Polar) to the original scan. Crop the image as shown.

There's something about the way all the tools arch their points toward the center that suggests a menacing intent (or is it just me?) They seem to be "looking" for a victim…so, I provided one. He's the "Cross-eyed" guy in the Digital Stock folder of the CD-ROM.

211

## Numeric Transform

☐ Position
H: [        ] [ pixels ▼ ]
V: [        ] [ pixels ▼ ]
    ☒ Relative

[ OK ]
[ Cancel ]

☒ Scale
Width: [ 60 ] [ percent ▼ ]
Height: [ 60 ] [ percent ▼ ]
    ☒ Constrain Proportions

☐ Skew
Horizontal: [        ] °
Vertical: [        ] °

☐ Rotate
Angle: [        ] °

**2** Drag and drop the victim to the Tools image, and turn the opacity of this new layer down to about 50% so you can see both layers. Reduce the victim's size to 60%, using Layer➡Transform➡Numeric.

**3** Make the Background layer invisible and erase everything on Layer 1 (the "victim" layer) except his face.

**4** Image➥Adjust➥Invert the colors of the layer to create a negative. The victim looks normal again in Step 5 (though he didn't look very normal to begin with).

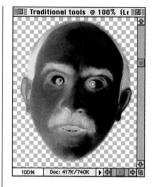

**5 Finally,** make the background layer visible and switch the "victim" layer (Layer 1) to Difference mode. This will make the inverted colors of the face go back to normal except where they are overlapped by the tools. ■

213

Here's a way to make the basic element of quilted upholstery. Use gradients and the Straight Line tool to construct the tile for a pattern fill.

**I** Switch to Default colors. Create a new file at 72 dpi. Mine is 4-inches square.

**2** Double-click the Line tool to open the Line Tool Options palette and match these settings. Hold down the Shift key to draw two perfect diagonals from corner to corner. The CMYK values for my salmon pink are 0, 62, 42, 0.

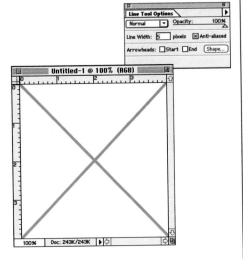

**3** Switch the foreground and background colors so that white is now the foreground and pink is the background.

**4** With the Magic Wand tool, click inside the left-hand white triangle to select it.

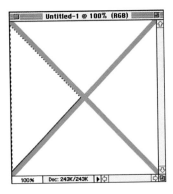

**5** Double-click the Gradient tool to open the Gradient Tool Options palette and match the settings shown here.

**6** Drag horizontally from the outside edge of the triangle to the center as accurately as you can.

 **Use the rulers to help make perfect fills that will result in a seamless pattern. (Command-R) [Control-R] toggles the rulers along the top and left side of the image. Begin your fill exactly at the 2-inch mark and hold down the Shift key for a perfect horizontal as you drag to the center.**

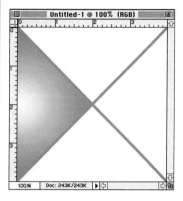

Repeat for each of the other triangles, blending from the middle of the outside edge to the center point. Your image should look like this:

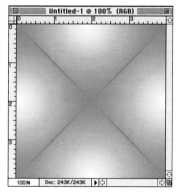

215

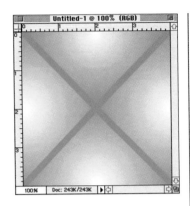

**7** I decided to strengthen the diagonal lines. It isn't necessary to redraw them. Just use the Magic Wand with a tolerance of 1 and click anywhere on the line. Both diagonals are selected. Select➡ Modify➡Expand by 1 pixel. If salmon pink is still your background color, press the Delete key and the pink lines become a bit fatter.

Now we want to create the button at the intersection of the diagonal lines. It is helpful to show the Grid and turn on Snap To Grid in the View menu.

**TIP** Use File➡Preferences➡ Guides & Grid to adjust grid units. My grid is set to show a gridline every inch and a subdivision every 1/4 inch.

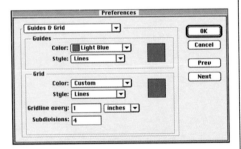

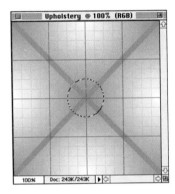

**8** Choose the elliptical Marquee tool. Place your cursor at the center of the image where the lines cross. Hold down the (Option-Shift)[Alt-Shift] keys while you drag outwards. You'll have a perfect circle perfectly centered.

**9** In the Gradient Tool Options palette, change the gradient type from Radial to Linear. Fill the circle with a gradient, using salmon pink as foreground color and white as background color. Drag the gradient from the lower-right to the upper-left of the circle. I dragged a little past the edge of the selection to get more pink and less white. This "button" should remain selected for the next Step.

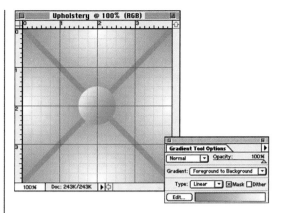

**10** Use the Move tool and the Option key to drag a copy of the button to each corner of the image. You want only a quadrant of the button to show. To make a seamless pattern, it's important to be accurate in placing these corner buttons.

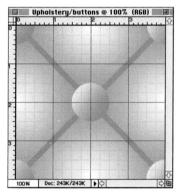

**11** Select Image➠Image Size Turn on Constrain proportions and Resample and change the 4-inch dimension to 2-inches.

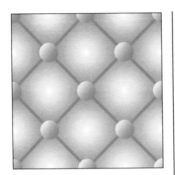

**12** Select all and choose
Edit➥Define Pattern. Now you can
fill any selected area with your
upholstery pattern by using
Edit➥Fill.

**TIP** Every time you use "Define
Pattern" the previous pattern is replaced. Save the
tile element from Step 11
as a separate file in case
you need it again.

## VARIATIONS

To make a rich velvet look, take the
pattern tile in Step 11 and convert
to Grayscale mode. Choose
Image➥Adjust➥Brightness/Contrast
(Brightness: -23, Contrast: +45).
Do Step 12 to establish this as your
current pattern.

Create a new file. Fill the image with red. I used CMYK values 2, 90, 32, 0. Repeat Step 9. Edit➡Fill using the new pattern element in Multiply mode, to allow the rich red virtual velvet to show through. How Victorian. ■

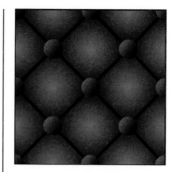

You can create beautiful effects without any raw material but your own ability to draw a straight line. If you are one of those people who "can't draw a straight line," Photoshop can do that for you, too.

**1** Create a new file. Mine is 4×2 inches.

**2** Double-click the Line tool to open the Line Tool Options palette and use these settings.

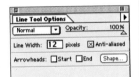

**3** Start near one of the upper corners of the image window and hold down the Shift key while you drag the line horizontally. This creates a perfectly horizontal black line with a thickness of 12 points.

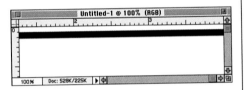

**4** Reduce the Line Width setting by 1 point, and begin drawing it below the first line, leaving enough space for a white stripe. Continue to reduce the thickness of stripes by 1 point until your image looks something like this.

**5** Drag a rectangular Marquee to select the stripes. Press and hold (Option-Command)[Alt-Control] and drag a copy of the stripes to the lower part of the image window. Allow this copy to remain a floating selection.

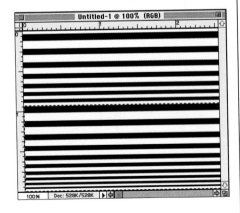

**6** Apply Layer➡Transform➡Flip
Vertical to the floating selection to
get a mirror image. You may have to
move the floating section into position with a few clicks on the keyboard arrows to get a perfect
match. It's OK if a couple of the
thinnest lines get "swallowed up" in
the process. Then deselect.

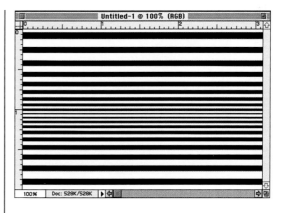

**7** Apply Filter➡Distort➡Twirl
(180).

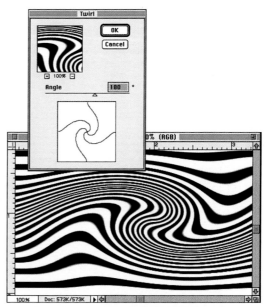

**8** I liked the results but I wanted to
have even more twirl, so I applied
the same distortion again, using the
(Command-F)[Control-F] shortcut.
This is the same as applying a 360
degree twirl in Step 7.

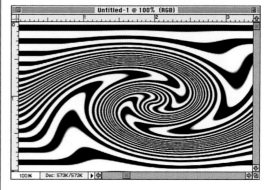

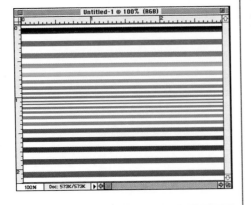

## VARIATIONS

Add color without affecting the white stripes by using Lighten mode with any of the painting tools or fill options.

Double-click the Gradient tool to open the Gradient Tool Options palette and use these settings to prepare for a multi-color fill that colors only the black pixels. Drag the gradient from top to bottom.

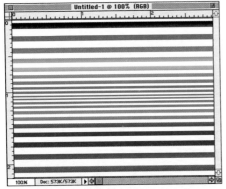

Here's a variation that began with the black stripes getting fatter toward the center of the image instead of thinner. Then I inverted the image to make white lines against a black background. The gradient style is radial this time, and the Darken mode was selected to pour color only into the white areas.

Throw caution to the wind and try drawing the lines freehand with the brush tool. I started with the brush in the first column of the second row in the Brushes palette, and for each successive line I selected the next larger size. Then I reversed the process to draw the bottom half of the image with the stripes getting thinner.

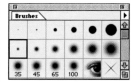

Even with a fairly steady hand, your lines will have a certain "organic" irregularity.

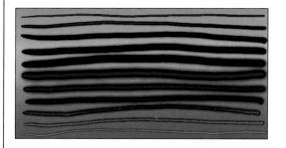

To colorize this variation, I used the violet, green, orange gradient, dragging from top to bottom. But this time I used Difference mode. A wonderful fuzzy glow results from the anti-aliased edges.

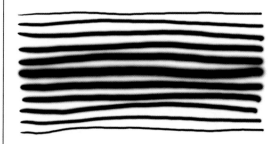

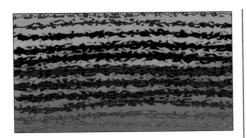

I applied Filter➡Distort➡Ocean Ripple (Size 7, Magnitude 7) to the previous image and got this psyche-delic seaweed thing. The possibilities are endless, so try the rest of the distort filters, and more! ∎

# Appendix A

## Contributor Listing

### Fonts

**Fonthead Design**         **(Mac and PC)**

1872-B Darryl Drive

Tallahassee, FL 32301-6017

ethan@fonthead.com

**Snyder Shareware Fonts**     **(Mac and PC)**

1797 Ross Inlet Road

Coos Bay, OR 97420

snyderrp@mail.coos.or.us  rps82@aol.com  76307.2431@compuserve.com

**Synstelien Design**         **(Mac and PC)**

1338 North 120th Plaza Apt#9

Omaha, NE 68154

Phone: 402-491-3065

http://www.synfonts.com

**Vintage Type**         **(Mac and PC)**

5662 Calle Real #146

Goleta CA 93117-2317

### Effects

**AutoFX**         **Sample Edge Effects (Mac and PC)**

15 North Main Street Suite 8

Wolfeboro, NH 03894

Phone: 603-569-8800

Fax: 603-569-9702

## Software & Filters

**Adobe Systems, Inc.**

345 Park Avenue

San Jose, CA 95110-6000

Phone: 408-536-6000

Fax: 408-537-6000

**Acrobat Reader™ 3.0 (Mac and PC)**

**Photoshop™ 3.0.5 Tryout (Mac and PC)**

**After Effects™ 3.0 Tryout (Mac only)**

**Streamline™ 3.1 Tryout (Mac and PC)**

**Dimensions™ 2.0 Tryout (Mac only)**

**Illustrator® 6.0 Tryout (Mac only)**

**Alien Skin Software**

1100 Wake Forest Rd. Suite 101

Raleigh, NC 27604

Phone: 919-832-4124

Fax: 919-832-4065

**Eye Candy 3.0 Demo (Mac and PC)**

**Andromeda Software, Inc.**

699 Hampshire Rd. Suite 109

Thousand Oaks, CA 91361

Phone: 800-547-0055 or 805-379-4109

Fax: 805-379-5253

orders@andromeda.com

**Series 1,2, & 3 Demos (Mac and PC)**

**Chris Cox**

110 Oakland Circle

Madison, AL 35758-8663

http://www.teleport.com/~ccox

**Chris's Filters 3.0 (Mac only)**

**DataStream Imaging Systems, Inc.**

P.O. Box 2148

Lexington, KY 40595-2148

800-889-7781 (Orders Only)

Phone: 606-264-0302

Fax: 606-263-0183

**Wild River SSK Demo (Mac only)**

**Fractal Design Corporation**

P.O. Box 66959

Scotts Valley, CA 95067-6959

Phone: 408-430-4000

http://www.fractal.com

**Jawai Interactive, Inc.**　　　　　**ScreenCaffeine Demo (Mac and PC)**

401 East Fourth Street Suite 443

Austin, TX 78701-3745

Phone: 800-600-6706 or 512-469-0502

Fax: 512-469-7850

info@jawai.com

**MetaTools, Inc.**　　　　　**KPT 3.0 Demo (Mac and PC)**

6303 Carpinteria Ave.

Carpinteria, CA 93013

805-566-6200

metasales@aol.com

**Neil Schulman**　　　　　**Frosty Filter (Mac only)**

**Specular, International**　　　　　**Infini-D™ Demo (Mac and PC)**

7 Pomeroy Lane　　　　　**Collage 2.0 Demo (Mac only)**

Amherst, MA 01002　　　　　**LogoMotion Demo (Mac only)**

Phone: 800-433-SPEC　　　　　**TextureScape™ Demo (Mac only)**

Fax: 413-253-0540

**Xaos Tools, Inc**　　　　　**Paint Alchemy 2™ Demo (Mac only)**

55 Hawthorn Suite 1000　　　　　**Terrazo 2™ Demo (Mac only)**

SanFrancisco, CA 94105　　　　　**TypeCaster™ Demo (Mac only)**

Phone: 1-800-BUY-XAOS

227

## Stock Images

### Digital Stock

400 S. Sierra Ave., Suite 100

Solana Beach, CA 92075

Phone: 619-794-4040 or 800-545-4514

Fax: 619-794-4041

### Image Club Graphics

729 24th Ave. SE

Calgary, AB, Canada

T2G 5K8

Phone: 403-262-8008 or 800-661-9410

Fax: 403-261-7013

http://www.adobe.com/imageclub

### PhotoDisc/CMCD

2013 Fourth Ave., 4th Floor

Seattle, WA 98121

Phone: 206-441-9355 or 800-528-3472

http://www.photodisc.com

# Appendix B

## What's on the CD-ROM

The CD-ROM that comes with this book is both Macintosh and Windows compatible. Please note that there are several demos and tryouts available for Macintosh users that are not available for Windows users, and vice versa. This means that either the product does not exist for that platform, or a version is being created but was not available at the time of publication.

We suggest that you refer to the READ ME and other information files included in the demo software program's folder. Also, visit the corporate Web sites for updates and more information. (The URLs are noted in Appendix A.) There are often demos of new software available for downloading and tryout.

The CD-ROM is divided into six folders. Macintosh folder names are in parentheses, and Windows folders are in brackets.

## Contents

### (Effects)[EFFECTS]

This is a collection of effects for manipulating images in Photoshop. Featured is a sampler of edge effects from AutoF/X.

### (Filters)

This folder contains lots of filters you can use to manipulate your images. You can do a variety of things with filters, one of the most powerful features of Photoshop. Some of these filters are freeware, some are shareware, and some are commercial demos.

### (Fonts)[FONTS]

Here you will find an excellent selection of shareware fonts to use in various effects.

### (Images)[IMAGES]

Many of the techniques in *Photoshop Effects Magic* begin with stock provided by commercial stock photo companies. You'll find them here, along with the ArtStart folder containing images prepared especially for this book.

### (Presets)[PRESETS]

Here's where you'll find the custom Brushes library and some extra displacement maps.

### (Software)[SOFTWARE]

This folder contains demos of commercial software, including Adobe products, and Fractal Design products.

### Installation

For detailed instructions on how to install and use the resources we've included on the CD-ROM, please consult the READ ME or ABOUT files in the individual software, filter, effects, and imagery folders. General installation information follows:

#### Filters

Filters should be copied into the Plug-Ins folder, located in the same place as your Adobe Photoshop application. Then, restart your computer, relaunch Photoshop, and find the filters in the Filter menu. You can now access and apply these third-party filters the same way you use Photoshop's filters.

#### Preset Files

The Magic Brushes library is a tiny file so you should copy it to your hard drive, into the same folder where your other Photoshop brushes are stored. You can access them with the Load Brushes command within Photoshop.

The dispmaps folder also contains a few small files, and they can be copied to the Displacement Maps folder using the same steps for copying Filters. None of these files is required for working a technique in the book.

#### Fonts (Macintosh)

Fonts should go in the Fonts folder, located in your System Folder. If you would like to try out a specific font, drag it to your closed System Folder. You should see a message stating that the fonts will be moved to the Fonts folder In the case of Type 1 fonts, you might need to drag multiple files to your System Folder.

#### Fonts (Windows)

Fonts should be installed by means of the Fonts Control Panel. Under Windows 95 or Windows NT 4.0 open Start menu➡Settings➡Control Panel➡Fonts. Then select File➡Install New Font… from the File menu and select the font from the CD-ROM that you want to install. The fonts can be found within the Fonts directory on the CD-ROM.

#### Stock imagery and textures

The stock photos and textures located in the Images folder do not need to be copied to your hard drive. For most files, you can double-click them to open them in Photoshop. If they do not, try opening Photoshop first, then select File➡Open. Then choose the file you want to open. If you particularly like a certain image and would like to access it quickly, by all means copy it to your hard drive.

## A Note About Shareware

If you use any shareware items beyond an initial trial period, you are obligated to follow the guidelines set forth by the author; this is usually in the form of a reasonable shareware payment. Your purchase of this book and the accompanying CD-ROM does not release you from this obligation. Refer to the READ ME and other information files that accompany each of the programs for specifics.

# Gallery

## Part I

*page 60*

*page 66*

*page 70*

*page 74*

*page 78*

*page 82*

*page 86*

*page 90*

*page 96*

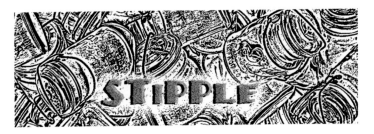

## Part II

*page 122*

*page 130*

*page 134*

*page 138*

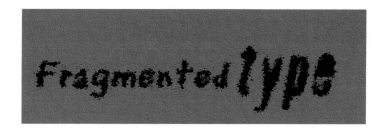

*page 142*

*page 146*

*page 150*

*page 156*

**Part III**

page 160

page 166

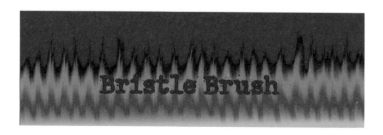

page 172

*page 190*

*page 194*

*page 198*

*textured Brush*

*page 214*

*page 220*

## Other DESIGN/GRAPHICS Titles

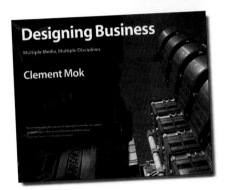

**Designing Business**

Provides the design/business communities with a new way of thinking about how the right design can be a strategic business advantage. It is the definitive guide to presenting a business identity through the use of traditional media vehicles and emerging technologies.

- CD-ROM (dual-platform) exhibits interactive prototypes of multimedia brochures, interactive television, and Web sites as developed by Clement Mok designs Inc., one of the most sought after interactive design agencies in the world
- Shows how effective communication is one way to out-think, out-plan, and out-perform the competition

*Clement Mok*
1-56830-282-7 ■ $60.00 USA/$81.95 CDN
264 pp., 8 x 10, Covers PC and Macintosh, New - Expert
*Available Now*

**Adobe Persuasion: Classroom in a Book**
1-56830-316-5 ■ $40.00 USA/$56.95 CDN
*Available November 1996*

**Learning Adobe FrameMaker**
1-56830-290-8 ■ $60.00 USA/$81.95 CDN
*Available Now*

**Adobe Illustrator for Windows: Classroom in a Book**
1-56830-053-0 ■ $44.95 USA/$59.99 CDN
*Available Now*

**Adobe Pagemaker for Windows: Classroom in a Book**
1-56830-184-7 ■ $45.00 USA/$61.95 CDN
*Available Now*

**Adobe Photoshop: Classroom in a Book**
1-56830-317-3 ■ $45.00 USA/$63.95 CDN
*Available October 1996*

**Advanced Adobe PageMaker for Windows 95: Classroom in a Book**
1-56830-262-2 ■ $50.00 USA/$68.95 CDN
*Available Now*

**Advanced Adobe Photoshop for Windows: Classroom in a Book**
1-56830-116-2 ■ $50.00 USA/$68.95 CDN
*Available Now*

**The Amazing PhotoDeluxe Book for Windows**
1-56830-286-X ■ $30.00 USA/$40.95 CDN
*Available Now*

**Branding with Type**
1-56830-248-7 ■ $18.00 USA/$24.95 CDN
*Available Now*

**The Complete Guide to Trapping, Second Edition**
1-56830-098-0 ■ $30.00 USA/$40.95 CDN
*Available Now*

**Design Essentials, Second Edition**
1-56830-093-X ■ $40.00 USA/$54.95 CDN
*Available Now*

**Digital Type Design Guide**
1-56830-190-1 ■ $45.00 USA/$61.95 CDN
*Available Now*

**Fractal Design Painter Creative Techniques**
1-56830-283-5 ■ $40.00 USA/$56.95 CDN
*Available Now*

**Photoshop Type Magic**
1-56830-220-7 ■ $35.00 USA/$47.95 CDN
*Available Now*

**Photoshop Type Magic 2**
1-56830-329-7 ■ $39.99 USA/$56.95 CDN
*Available November 1996*

**Adobe Photoshop Complete**
1-56830-323-8 ■ $45.00 USA/$61.95 CDN
*Available October 1996*

**Production Essentials**
1-56830-124-3 ■ $40.00 USA/$54.95 CDN
*Available Now*

**Stop Stealing Sheep & find out how type works**
0-672-48543-5 ■ $19.95 USA/$26.99 CDN
*Available Now*

**Visit your fine local bookstore, or for more information visit us at http//:www.mcp.com/hayden**

# REGISTRATION CARD

Hayden
Books

## Photoshop Effects Magic

Name _____ Title _____

Company_____Type of business _____

Address _____

City/State/ZIP _____

Have you used these types of books before?  ☐ yes  ☐ no

If yes, which ones? _____

_____

How many computer books do you purchase each year?  ☐ 1–5  ☐ 6 or more

How did you learn about this book? _____

☐ recommended by a friend                    ☐ received ad in mail
☐ recommended by store personnel            ☐ read book review
☐ saw in catalog                             ☐ saw on bookshelf

Where did you purchase this book? _____

Which applications do you currently use? _____

Which computer magazines do you subscribe to? _____

What trade shows do you attend? _____

Please number the top three factors which most influenced your decision for this book purchase.

☐ cover                      ☐ price
☐ approach to content        ☐ author's reputation
☐ logo                       ☐ publisher's reputation
☐ layout/design              ☐ other _____

Would you like to be placed on our preferred mailing list?  ☐ yes  ☐ no  e-mail address _____

---

☐ **I would like to see my name in print!** You may use my name and quote me in future Hayden products and promotions. My daytime phone number is: _____

---

Comments _____

_____

_____

## Hayden Books   Attn: Product Marketing ◆ 201 West 103rd Street ◆ Indianapolis, Indiana 46290  USA

Fax to **317-581-3576**          Visit out Web Page **http://WWW.MCP.com/hayden/**

Fold Here

## BUSINESS REPLY MAIL

**FIRST-CLASS MAIL PERMIT NO. 9918 INDIANAPOLIS IN**

POSTAGE WILL BE PAID BY THE ADDRESSEE

**HAYDEN BOOKS**
**Attn: Product Marketing**
**201 W 103RD ST**
**INDIANAPOLIS IN 46290-9058**

MACMILLAN COMPUTER PUBLISHING USA

A VIACOM COMPANY

## Technical ----- Support:

If you cannot get the CD/Disk to install properly, or you need
assistance with a particular situation in the book, please feel
free to check out the Knowledge Base on our Web site at
**http://www.superlibrary.com/general/support**. We have
answers to our most Frequently Asked Questions listed there.
If you do not find your specific question answered, please
contact Macmillan Technical Support at **(317) 581-3833**.
We can also be reached by email at **support@mcp.com**.